CRASH COURSE
Windows 95 & NT 4.0

For the busy person on the job

Joel Murach

Mike Murach & Associates
2560 West Shaw Lane, Suite 101
Fresno, California 93711-2765
(209) 275-3335

Author:	Joel Murach
Editor:	Anne Prince
Cover Design:	Zylka Design
Interior design:	Shields Design
Production:	Tom Murach

Other books that use the same presentation methods

Crash Courses:	A Crash Course in Word 95
	A Crash Course in Excel 95
Windows 95 books:	Work like a PRO with Word for Windows 95
	Work like a PRO with Excel for Windows 95
Word 6 books:	Work like a PRO with Word 6 for Windows
	Word 6: How to use the Mail Merge Feature
Excel 5 books:	Work like a PRO with Excel 5 for Windows
	Excel 5: Lists, Pivot Tables & External Databases

© 1997, Mike Murach & Associates, Inc.
All rights reserved.
Printed in the United States of America.

10 9 8 7 6 5 4 3 2 1
ISBN: 0-911625-97-6

Contents

Chapter 1

Essential Windows skills

An introduction to Windows 95 & NT 4	2
How to log on	2
The desktop	3
How to perform the six basic mouse actions	4
How to use the Start menu	5
How to shut down your computer	6

How to work with windows	8
Window concepts and terms	8
How to open a window	9
How to switch from one window to another	10
How to minimize, maximize, restore, or close a window	11
How to move or size a window	12
How to scroll through the contents of a window	13

How to work with menus and commands	16
How to issue a command from a pull-down menu	16
How to use shortcut menus	17
How to work with a dialog box	18
Keyboard techniques for working with dialog boxes	19
How to work with dialog boxes that contains tabs	20
How to use the Exit command	20

How to work with folders and files	22
How to use the standard Open command	24
How to select a drive and folder in a dialog box	25
How to select a file in a dialog box	26
How to use the standard Save As command	27
How to manage folders and files from a dialog box	28
How to manage folders and files with the Windows Explorer	29
How to work with the Recycle Bin	30
How to find folders and files	31

Perspective
Summary

Chapter 2

11 more skills and the Help feature

Eleven more Windows skills	36
How to use shortcuts on your desktop	36
How to add shortcuts to your desktop	37
How to add shortcuts to the top of the Start menu	38
How to organize your Start menu	39
How to control the view in folder windows	40
How to work with the Control Panel	41
How to work with local drives	42
How to work with network drives	43
How to share local files and printers	44
How to work with printers	45
How to manage the print queue	46

When and how to get online help	47
How to use the Help Topics dialog box	47
How to work with a Help topic	48
How to get help from a dialog box	49

Perspective
Summary

Introduction

The books in our Crash Course series are designed for busy people on the job who need to be accomplished PC users, but don't have time for 4-hour courses or 500-page books. That makes our Crash Courses the right books for people who need to upgrade or convert to a new program as quickly as possible; the right books for people who have marginal PC skills and want to improve them; and the right books for novices too.

What this book does

This book is designed to teach you the Windows 95 or Windows NT 4.0 skills that you need on the job every day. If you are upgrading or converting to Windows 95 or NT 4.0, this book is intended to get you back to where you were before you upgraded or converted...and it's designed to do that in just an hour or two. So when you're done with this book, you'll be able to:

- ✓ start and use your old application programs with Windows 95 or NT 4.0
- ✓ use the Open and Save commands of any program that's designed for use with Windows 95 or NT 4.0
- ✓ use the Explorer to manage files and folders
- ✓ organize your Windows desktop for efficient use
- ✓ use the new Help features to learn any other Windows skills that you need (if and when you decide that you need any)

If you're wondering how Windows 95 and NT 4.0 can be treated in the same book, it's because the user interface is the same for both versions of Windows. In other words, the functions that are summarized above work the same on both versions of Windows. In fact, many people believe that Windows 95 and Windows NT will eventually be combined into a single system.

3 ways this book differs from all the others

- ✓ In this one short book, you can learn all of the skills that the typical Windows user needs on the job. We know because everyone in our company uses Windows 95 or Windows NT 4.0. And this book presents all the skills that we require.
- ✓ Each skill is presented in a single figure on the right side of a page. This figure illustrates the Windows feature and summarizes all the essential information for using it effectively. This is the most efficient presentation method that we've seen to date, and no one else has anything like it.
- ✓ In case you need them, the first chapter also includes practice exercises. Unlike the exercises in other books, though, these exercises don't just walk you through a lockstep procedure. Instead, they show you the most efficient ways to do functions and encourage you to try new functions. As you do the exercises, you'll see that you really can master Windows with nothing more than this book to assist you.

Now, think for a moment about these differences. With this book, you'll use a skill-based presentation method to learn everything you need to know about Windows in just 50 pages. And if you have trouble getting started, the exercises are there to help you build your confidence.

The end result is that you'll learn faster and retain more. And when you're done using this book for learning, it becomes the quickest on-the-job reference you'll ever use. Look up the skill or function you need in the index; find the page it's on; and get all the information you need in the one figure on that page.

Your comments, please

If you have any comments about this book, we would enjoy hearing from you. Did this book help you get started quickly with a minimum of frustration? Have you been able to find out how to do new functions in 5 minutes or less? Has the book helped you become a more accomplished Windows user? Good or bad, we need to know how the book worked for you.

So if you have any comments, criticism, or praise, please use the postage-paid form at the back of this book. As always, our goal is not only to help you get the most from your software, but also to help you do that as quickly and easily as possible. And thanks for trying this book.

Mike Murach
Publisher

Chapter 1

Essential Windows skills

This chapter presents the essential skills for working with Windows 95 or Windows NT 4.0. In general, though, these skills are exactly the same for both versions of Windows. As a result, this book only refers to Windows NT 4 (or NT 4) on those few occasions when there is a slight difference in the way a skill is done. Otherwise, any reference to Windows 95 can also be interpreted as a reference to Windows NT 4.

As you go through this chapter, you'll see that each set of skills is followed by exercises that are designed to get you started right. These exercises require nothing but this book, your PC, Windows 95 or NT 4, and one application program that was designed to run under Windows 95 and NT 4. Although the exercises use Word 95 as that application program, you can substitute the use of another application program if you don't have Word 95 on your system.

Of course, you may decide to skip the exercises and experiment on your own. But if you have any trouble with the skills in this chapter, please do the exercises. They show you how to apply the skills that are presented in the figures, and they can be an important part of the learning process.

An introduction to Windows 95 & NT 4 2
How to log on 2
The desktop 3
How to perform the six basic mouse actions 4
How to use the Start menu 5
How to shut down your computer 6

How to work with windows 8
Window concepts and terms 8
How to open a window 9
How to switch from one window to another 10
How to minimize, maximize, restore, or close a window 11
How to move or size a window 12
How to scroll through the contents of a window 13

How to work with menus and commands 16
How to issue a command from a pull-down menu 16
How to use shortcut menus 17
How to work with a dialog box 18
Keyboard techniques for working with dialog boxes 19
How to work with dialog boxes that contain tabs 20
How to use the Exit command 20

How to work with folders and files 22
How to use the standard Open command 24
How to select a drive and folder in a dialog box 25
How to select a file in a dialog box 26
How to use the standard Save As command 27
How to manage folders and files from a dialog box 28
How to manage folders and files with the Windows Explorer 29
How to work with the Recycle Bin 30
How to find folders and files 31

Perspective
Summary

An introduction to Windows 95 & NT 4

When you first begin working with Windows 95 or NT 4, there are a handful of skills that you'll need to learn to get started. Those skills include how to start Windows and how to shut down your computer.

How to log on

Windows 95 and Windows NT 4 are both designed to start automatically when you turn on your PC. As Windows starts, a logo screen is displayed followed by an hourglass that indicates that the startup procedure is in progress. During this procedure, Windows may display a dialog box that asks you to *log on*.

Figure 1-1 shows two of the formats that the dialog box for logging on may take. This format depends on the type of network you're using and how that network is set up. No matter what the format is, though, you usually just have to enter your password because the correct entries for name and domain are already there. Once you're logged on, a desktop like the one in figure 1-2 is displayed.

The primary reason to log on is so you can use a *network*. When you're logged on to the network, you can access files, printers, and other network resources that are located on other PCs on the network. In most companies, you will have to get a valid name and password from the system or network administrator before you can use the network.

A dialog box for logging on to Windows

A dialog box for logging on to a network

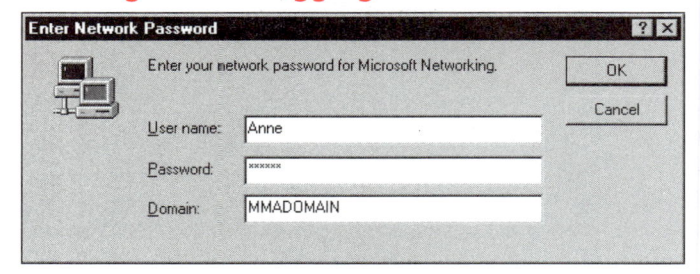

How to log on to Windows 95

- Enter your user name (if it isn't already correct), your password, and your *domain* (if necessary). To move from one text box to the next, press the Tab key. When the entries are correct, press the Enter key.

How to log on to Windows NT

1. When the Begin Logon dialog box is displayed, press Ctrl+Alt+Delete to begin the log on procedure.
2. When the Logon Information dialog box is displayed, enter your user name (if it isn't already correct), your password, and your *domain* (if necessary). To move from one text box to the next, press the Tab key. When the entries are correct, press the Enter key.

Notes

- If necessary, get an appropriate user name and password from your company's network administrator. You may also have to find out what domain your account is in.
- Capitalization matters when you enter your password so be sure to enter it correctly. If the password doesn't work, you should check to make sure that Caps Lock isn't on.
- Some log on procedures provide access to a user profile. For more information about user profiles, look up "user profiles" in the online Help index (see chapter 2).

Figure 1-1   How to log on

Chapter 1   Essential Windows skills   3

A secondary reason to log on is to access a *user profile*. A user profile contains a variety of settings that can affect the appearance and contents of the Windows display. User profiles are used most often when two or more people use the same PC. Then, each user can have a different user profile that provides a customized display. However, a single user can also have more than one user profile.

When you use Windows 95, you might not be required to log on. In that case, the display in figure 1-2 appears without any intervening dialog boxes. And if you don't want to attach to a network or access a user profile, you can press the Esc key to skip the dialog box that lets you log on.

The desktop

The first time you start Windows 95 or NT 4, the starting display will look something like the one shown in figure 1-2. This display is called the *desktop*. In this example, the desktop contains the *taskbar*, the Microsoft Office Shortcut Bar, and five *icons*. Your display will vary depending on the programs that are installed on your PC. If Microsoft Office isn't installed, for example, the Microsoft Office Shortcut Bar won't be available.

Your desktop may also be customized so that it contains features not shown in figure 1-2. For example, it may contain one or more *shortcut icons* that let you quickly access the resources you need (see chapter 2). Or, it may be set up so that the programs you use most are started automatically when you start Windows. As a result, the starting display in school or business may look quite different from the one in figure 1-2.

A simple desktop

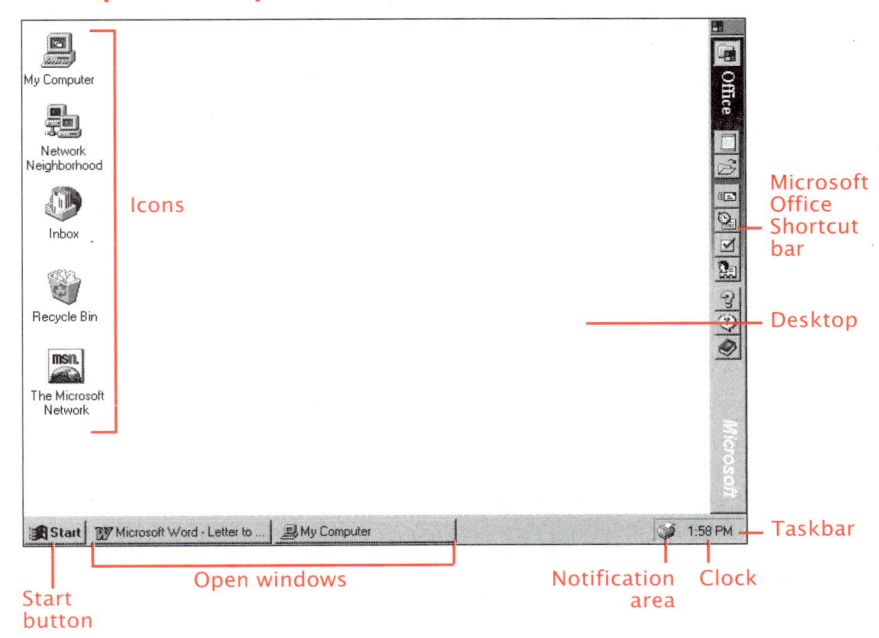

Concepts and terms

- The *desktop* is the backdrop that all other Windows components are displayed on. In the screen shown above, the desktop contains the *taskbar*, the Microsoft Office Shortcut Bar, and five *icons*.
- The taskbar contains the Start button, one button for each open window, the *notification area*, and the *clock*. By default, the taskbar is displayed at the bottom of the screen as shown above.
- The Start button can be used to display a menu that lets you perform a variety of functions, as summarized in figure 1-4.
- The icons on the desktop can represent folders, documents, programs, or printers. The three most common icons are My Computer, Network Neighborhood, and Recycle Bin. My Computer is a folder that contains all the other folders and files on your PC. Network Neighborhood is a folder that contains all the resources that are available on your network (if you're connected to one). And Recycle Bin is a folder that contains deleted files (see figure 1-25).

Note

- Because the Windows desktop can be customized in many ways, your desktop probably won't look like the one shown above. In particular, your desktop may contain *shortcuts* that appear as icons on the desktop. Shortcut icons make it easy to start programs and access documents you use frequently (see chapter 2).

Figure 1-2   **The desktop**

How to perform the six basic mouse actions

Windows was designed for use with a mouse. That's why you can perform many functions more quickly with a mouse than you can with the keyboard.

To use a mouse with Windows, you need to master the six basic mouse actions that are summarized in figure 1-3. Although these actions may seem difficult if you haven't used a mouse before, you'll quickly become adept at using them.

As you work with Windows 95 or NT 4, you'll find that it has been designed to make more use of the right mouse button. Because of that, it's important for you to distinguish between actions that use the left and right buttons. Throughout this book, click, drag, and double-click will refer to actions that use the left mouse button. If you need to use the right mouse button, we'll tell you specifically to right-click or right-drag. Of course, if you're left-handed, you'll want to set up your mouse so that the button functions are reversed.

The dialog box you can use to set up your mouse

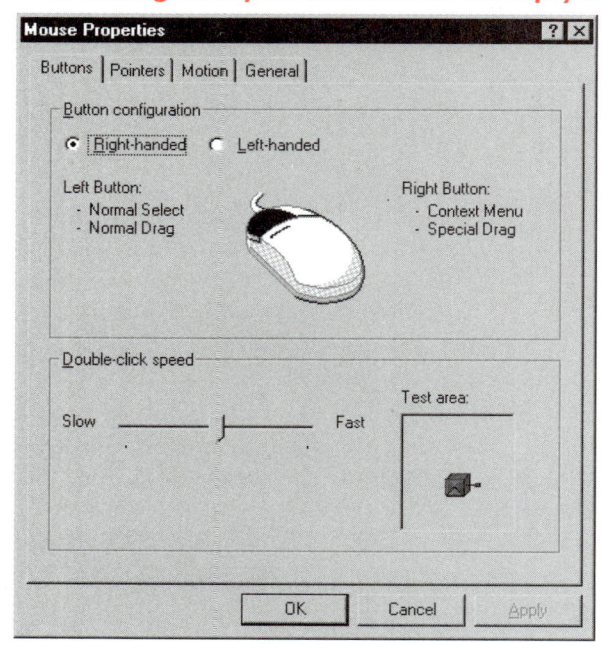

The six basic mouse actions

Action	How to do it
Point	Move the mouse so the mouse pointer is positioned on the object that you're interested in.
Click	Without moving the mouse pointer off the object you're pointing to, press and release the left mouse button so it clicks.
Drag	After you point to an object, press and hold down the left mouse button, move the mouse pointer to a new location, then release the left mouse button.
Double-click	Without moving the mouse pointer off the object you're pointing to, press and release the left mouse button twice in succession. Do this quickly, in less than a second.
Right-click	Without moving the mouse pointer off the object you're pointing to, press and release the right mouse button so it clicks.
Right-drag	After you point to an object, press and hold down the right mouse button, move the mouse pointer to a new location, then release the right mouse button.

How to change the mouse buttons for left-handed use

- If you're left-handed, you can use the Mouse icon in the Control Panel window to access the dialog box shown above. The Control Panel is a Windows feature that works much the same as it did with Windows 3.1 (do exercise set 2 or see chapter 2).

Figure 1-3   How to perform the six basic mouse actions

How to use the Start menu

Windows provides a variety of techniques for starting programs, changing system settings, and performing other system functions. One way is to use the Start menu, which is summarized in figure 1-4. To access this menu, you click on the Start button in the taskbar.

In this chapter, you'll learn how to use the Start menu to open program and document windows, find folders and files, and shut down your PC. But as you can see from figure 1-4, there's a lot more you can do from the Start menu. When you finish this chapter, you'll have the skills to use these other functions.

The Start menu with the Settings submenu displayed

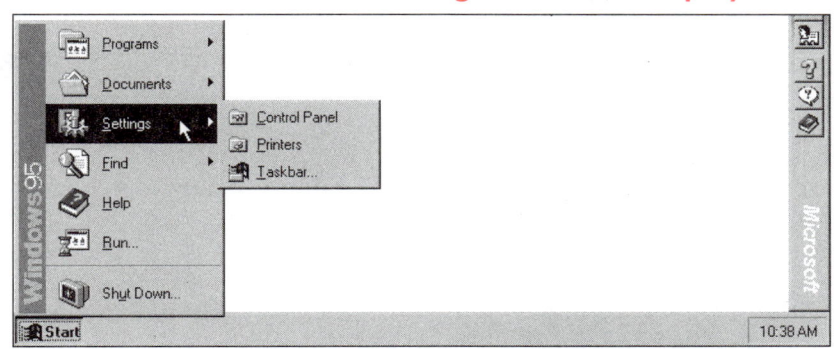

How to use the Start menu

- To display the Start menu, click on the Start button at the left side of the taskbar.
- To issue the Help, Run, or Shut Down command, click on the appropriate menu item.
- To display the Programs, Documents, Settings, or Find *submenu*, point to the appropriate menu item. To issue a command from a submenu, click on it.

A summary of the commands in the Start menu

Command	Description
Programs	Displays a list of the programs you can start from this menu. See figure 1-7 for details.
Documents	Displays a list of the last 15 documents you used and lets you open them. A document is any file created by a program.
Settings	Lets you change the settings for a variety of system components.
Find	Lets you find a folder or file.
Help	Accesses online Help for Windows 95 or NT 4. See figures 2-12 and 2-13 in chapter 2 for details.
Run	Lets you start a program or open a folder or document by typing its name.
Shut Down	Lets you shut down or restart your computer. See figure 1-5 for details.

Notes

- If the taskbar is hidden from view, you can display the Start menu by pressing press Ctrl+Esc.
- To exit from the Start menu or any of its submenus without issuing a command, click anywhere outside the menu. To close one menu at a time, press the Esc key.
- See figure 1-12 for other techniques for working with menus.

Figure 1-4   How to use the Start menu

How to shut down your computer

Figure 1-5 shows how to use the Shut Down command in the Start menu to shut down your computer. When you issue this command, you're presented with at least the first two options. You use the first option to shut down your PC so it's safe to turn it off. You use the second option to restart or *reboot* your computer.

The third option will only be available to you if you are using Windows 95. You can use it to restart your computer in MS-DOS mode. If you're completely new to PCs, you may not know that DOS is the Disk Operating System that has been used to run most PCs since the early 1980s. MS-DOS is the Microsoft version of this operating system. Since you can run DOS programs without leaving Windows, you will only need to use the DOS mode if you have a DOS program that won't run properly under Windows 95.

The Windows 95 dialog box that's displayed before your computer is shut down

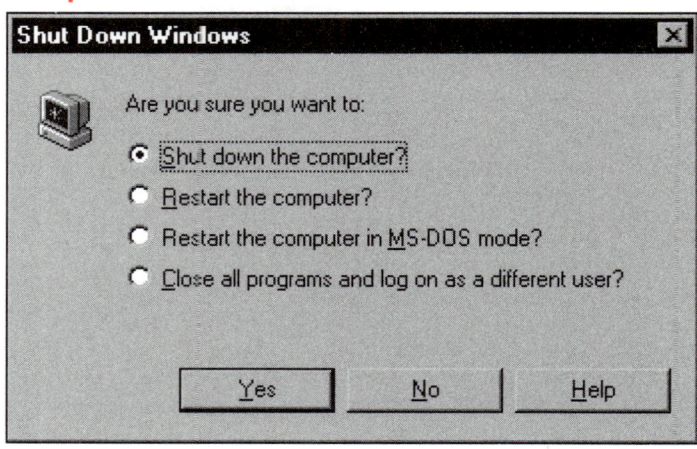

How to shut down your computer

1. Click on the Start button to display the Start menu.
2. Click on the Shut Down command to display the dialog box shown above.
3. Click on the Yes button to shut down your computer. During the shutdown process, Windows attempts to close any open programs and save changes to any open documents. In some cases, you may be prompted for additional information.
4. When you're prompted by Windows, turn off your computer.

How to use the other options in the Shut Down Windows dialog box

- The Restart the Computer option lets you restart your computer without turning the power off, then back on again. You may want to use this option if you change any system settings that affect the way your computer operates.
- The Close All Programs option lets another user log on without having to shut down or restart the computer. This option is only available if your computer is connected to a network or if it's set up to provide for two or more user profiles.
- The Restart the Computer in MS-DOS Mode option is only available if you're using Windows 95. It restarts the computer and displays a DOS prompt. You may need to use this option to run a DOS program that won't run under Windows 95. To start Windows from the DOS prompt, type "win" or "exit" and press the Enter key.

Notes

- If you decide that you don't want to shut down or restart your computer, click on the No button in the Shut Down Windows dialog box or press the Esc key when this dialog box is displayed. Then, you're returned to your Windows session.
- If your PC has frozen, you can press Ctrl+Alt+Delete to access a dialog box that contains buttons that let you close programs and, if necessary, shut down your system.

Figure 1-5   How to shut down your computer

Exercise set 1

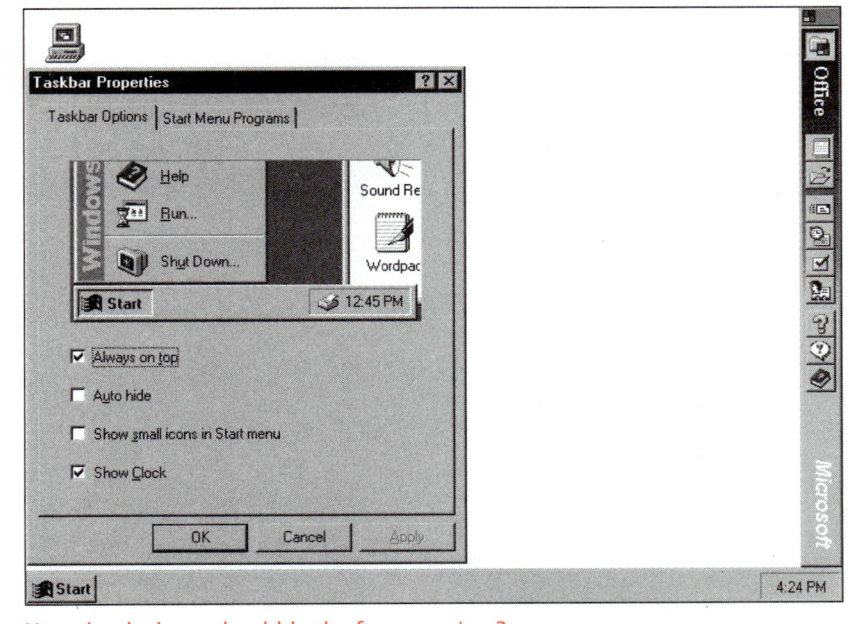

How the desktop should look after exercise 3

The exercises that follow are designed to get you started with Windows and familiarize you with the desktop.

1. Start your PC. Do you get a dialog box that asks for your user name and password? If so, respond to the dialog box as described in figure 1-1. When the startup procedure finishes, you should see your desktop. If any program or folder windows are open, you'll need to click the right mouse button on a blank area of the taskbar to display a menu and then click on the Minimize All Windows command so you can see the desktop.

2. Is the taskbar displayed at the bottom of the screen? If it's displayed anywhere else, place the mouse pointer over a blank portion of the taskbar and drag it to the bottom of your screen. If you can't see the taskbar, move the mouse pointer to the bottom, top, left, and right of the screen until the taskbar is displayed. Is the clock area displayed in the taskbar? If so, use the mouse to point to it. Is the correct time displayed?

3. Click on the Start button to display the Start menu. Point to the Settings menu item to display the menu shown in figure 1-4, then click on the Taskbar command. Your screen should now look like the one shown above.

4. Look at the options that are displayed on the screen. If the Auto Hide option has a check mark in front of it, click on it to remove the check mark. (If this option is checked, the taskbar is only displayed if you point to it.) If the Show Clock option does not have a check mark in front of it, click on it to check it. Then, click on the OK button to save any changes you made.

5. Display the Start menu again, then click on the Shut Down command to display a dialog box like the one in figure 1-5. If you're ready to end your Windows session, shut down your computer using the procedure in figure 1-5. Otherwise, click on the No button or press the Esc key to cancel the operation and continue working with Windows.

How to work with windows

One of the benefits that you get from using Windows is that you can have more than one task running at the same time. Each active task runs in its own *window*. After you open the windows you want to use, you can quickly switch between them. You can also use the controls in a window to minimize, maximize, restore, close, and scroll through the window. And you can move and size a window.

Window concepts and terms

Figure 1-6 illustrates the three types of windows you'll use as you work with Windows 95 or NT 4. A *program window*, also called an *application window*, contains a program. A *document window*, which is always within a program window, provides a work space that's used by the program. In the first example in figure 1-6, the program window contains Word and the document window contains a letter. In contrast, a *folder window* like the My Computer window in the second example contains icons that represent the drives, folders, and files available to your PC.

As you can see, all three types of windows have a *title bar*. However, only program windows and folder windows have a *menu bar*. You use the menu bar in the program window to work with the document in the document window.

The program window and a document window for Word

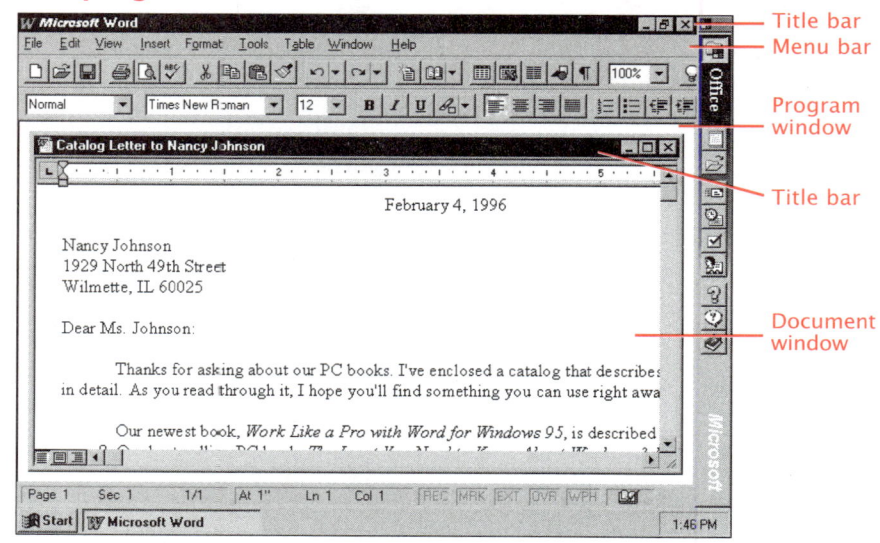

The folder window for My Computer

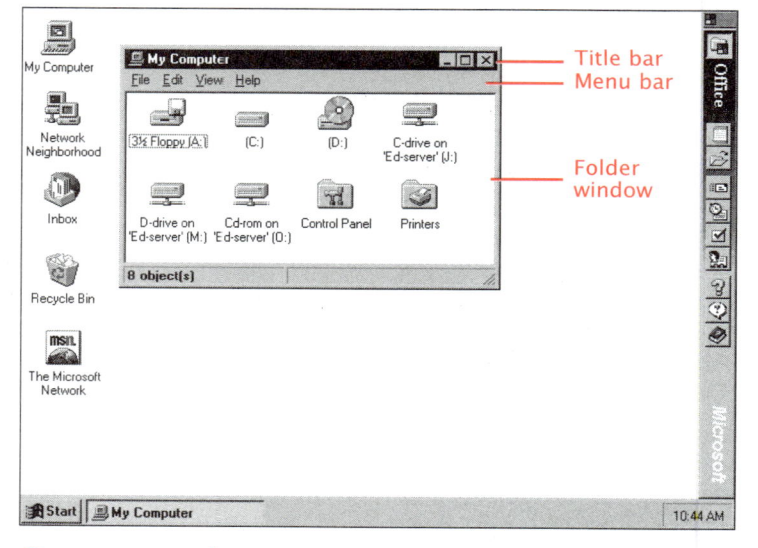

Concepts and terms

- A program runs in a *program window*. A *document window* provides a work space for the program in the program window, and it's always within the program window. A *folder window* can contain drives, folders, and files.
- The *title bar* gives the name of a program, document, or folder.
- A *menu bar* appears in program and folder windows. It provides the menus that list the commands you can use in that window.

Figure 1-6   Window concepts and terms

How to open a window

Figure 1-7 presents the techniques for opening folder, program, and document windows. To open a folder window, you can double-click on a *folder icon*. Some folder icons, like My Computer, Network Neighborhood, and Recycle Bin, appear on the desktop. Other folder icons appear within folder windows, as you can see in this figure. You can also double-click on a *drive icon* like those shown in the figure 1-7 to open a folder window.

The techniques you can use to open program and document windows depend on how your desktop is set up. If, for example, you've added a shortcut icon for a program to your desktop, you can double-click on that icon to start the program. Or, if you've added a document to the top of the Start menu, you can click on that menu item to open the document. No matter how your desktop is set up, though, you can always use the Start menu to open program and document windows as described in figure 1-7.

When you use the Start menu to open a program window or a document window, you should realize that both types of windows are opened. When you use the technique for opening a program window, a blank document window is opened within the program window. Then, you can use the program's Open command to open the document you want to work on. When you use the technique for opening a document window, a program window for the program associated with the document is opened first. Then, the document window is opened and the document you selected is opened into the window.

The Start menu with the Programs and Microsoft Office submenus displayed over the folder window for My Computer

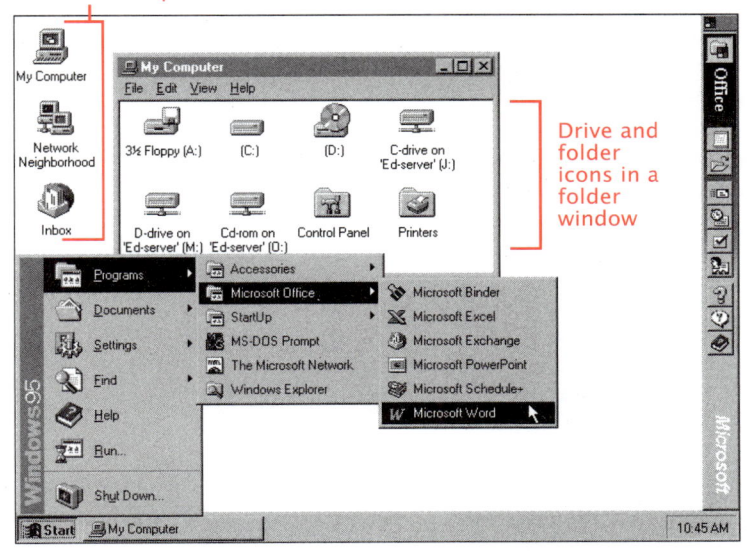

How to open a folder window

- Double-click on a *folder icon* on the desktop (like My Computer, Network Neighborhood, or Recycle Bin) or on a folder icon within another folder window. Double-clicking on a *drive icon* also opens a folder window.

How to open a program window using the Start menu

- Click on a program in the Programs menu or any of its submenus. A program window is opened with a blank document window.

How to open a document window using the Start menu

- Click on a document in the Documents menu or any of its submenus. A document window that contains the selected document is opened within a program window for the program that's associated with the document.

Other ways to open program and document windows

- Double-click on a *shortcut icon* for a program or document that's displayed on the desktop.
- Click on a program or document menu item that's been added to the top of the Start menu.
- Click on the Start a New Document or Open a Document button in the Microsoft Office Shortcut bar.
- Double-click on a file icon in a folder window.

Note

- When you open a window, a button for that window is displayed on the taskbar.

Figure 1-7   How to open a window

How to switch from one window to another

If two or more windows are open at the same time, you can use the techniques in figure 1-8 to switch between them. The fastest way to switch between windows is by clicking on the appropriate taskbar button. You can also use Alt+Tab switching to switch between windows, just as you did in Windows 3.1. Note that Alt+Tab switching will work even if the taskbar is hidden.

If two or more windows are displayed at the same time as in figure 1-8, the title bar of the active window is always highlighted. In addition, the active window is usually the one on top. However, some windows, such as the ones that contain Help information, are designed to stay on top even when they aren't active.

The taskbar with buttons for two open windows

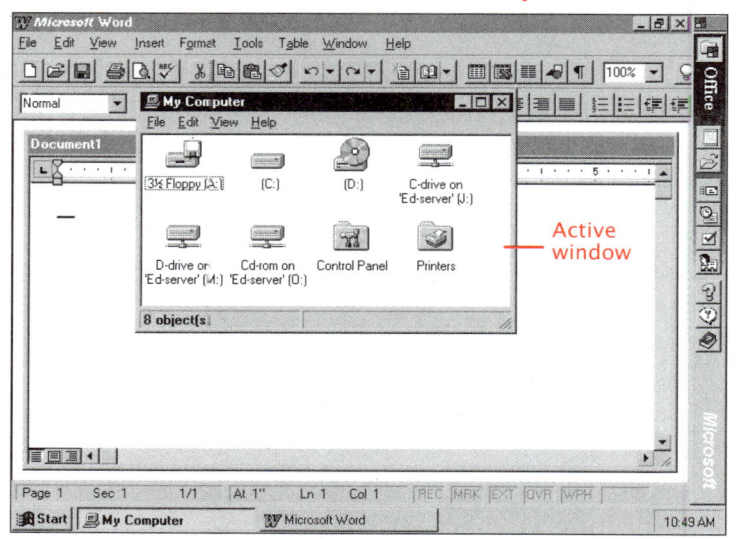

How to use the taskbar
- Click on the taskbar button for a window to switch to that window.
- If the text on a taskbar button is truncated, you can point to the button to display its complete text.

How to use Alt+Tab switching
1. Hold down the Alt key and press the Tab key to display a panel that contains an icon for each window that's open. The name of the next window in sequence is displayed at the bottom of the panel.
2. If that isn't the window that you want to switch to, press the Tab key again while you continue to hold down the Alt key. When the name of the window you want to switch to is displayed, release the Alt key. Or, to cancel the switch, press the Esc key while still holding down the Alt key.

How to switch when two or more windows are displayed at the same time
- Click on any part of a window to switch to it.

How to display the taskbar
- If the taskbar isn't displayed, choose the Taskbar command from the Settings submenu of the Start menu. In the Taskbar Properties dialog box that's displayed, click on the Always on Top option to place a check mark in front of it. Then, click on the OK button to save the change. (If the Auto Hide option has a check mark in front of it, the taskbar is only displayed when you point to its location.)

Figure 1-8 How to switch from one window to another

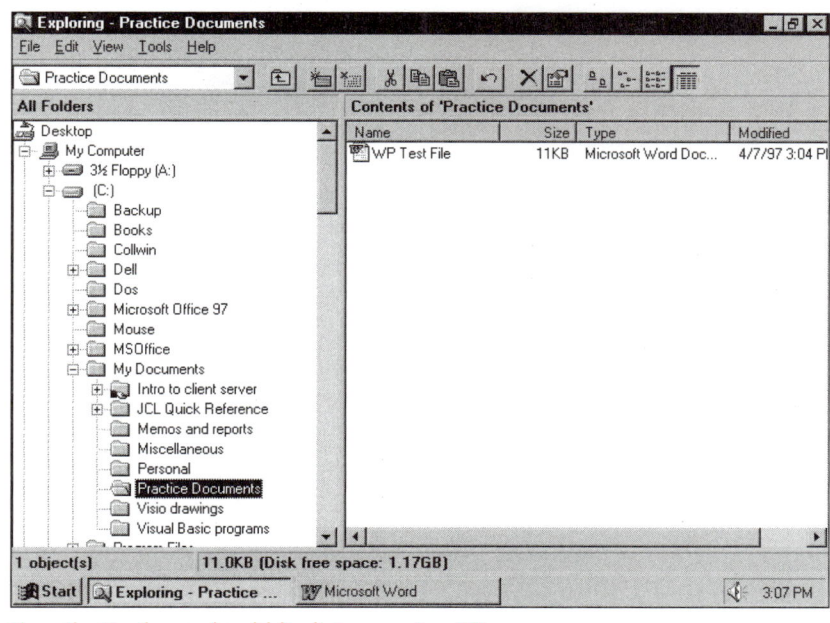

How the Explorer should look in exercise 10

10. Switch to the Explorer window. Then, find the Practice Documents folder in the left pane and click on its icon to show its contents in the right pane. There, you should see the name of the file that you created in exercise 8 as shown above.

11. Right-click on WP Test File, choose the Delete command, and confirm the deletion if necessary. Then, right-click on the Practice Documents folder in the left pane, press the Delete key, and confirm the deletion if necessary. Both the file and the folder that you created are now deleted.

12. Scroll through the folders in the left pane until you see the Recycle Bin folder and click on it. Then, locate WP Test File in the right pane, right click on it, and choose the Restore command. To see that both the file and its folder have been restored, find the Practice Documents folder again and click on it.

13. Use the procedure in figure 1-26 to find any file on the C drive that has "test" in its file name. To do that, just type *test* in the Named box. In the list of the files that are found, find WP Test File and double-click on its name to open it. This switches you back to your word processing program.

14. Close WP Test File. Next, issue the Open command, and delete both WP Test File and the Practice Documents folder using either the shortcut menus or the Delete key. Then, click on the Cancel button to close the dialog box, and close all open windows.

Perspective

This chapter has presented the minimum set of skills you need to get started. Because this chapter has presented so much information, though, you may be slightly overwhelmed by it...especially if you're new to PCs or Windows.

In practice, though, the only skills that continue to give people trouble are those for working with folders and files. So if you're uneasy about those skills, you may want to go through exercise set 4 again. In particular, you should make sure that you know how to select a folder as you open or save a file. Once you're confident that you can do that, you're ready to learn the Windows 95 and NT 4 skills presented in chapter 2, and you're ready for application programs like Word and Excel.

Summary

- When you start Windows 95 or Windows NT 4, you may need to supply a user name and password to *log on* to Windows with a *user profile* or to log on to a *network*.

- The Windows 95 and NT 4 *desktop* contains at least these three *icons*: My Computer, Network Neighborhood, and Recycle Bin. These icons represent folders that contain other folders, files, and system resources.

- By default, the *taskbar* is displayed across the bottom of the desktop.

- To use the mouse, you need to know the six basic mouse actions: *point*, *click*, *double-click*, *drag*, *right-click,* and *right-drag*.

- When you start a program, a *program window* is opened for it. Within this program window, a program creates its own work spaces called *document windows*. Windows 95 and NT 4 also use *folder windows*, which let you work with the *drives*, *folders*, and *files* on your PC.

- You can *maximize, minimize, restore,* or *close* a window by clicking on its Maximize, Minimize, Restore, or Close button. When a program or folder window is minimized, you can click on its taskbar button to restore it.

- When a window is too small to show all of its contents, *scroll bars* are added to it. Then, you can use the mouse to scroll through the window by clicking on the scroll bar or *scroll arrows* or by dragging the *scroll box*.

- You can use either mouse or keyboard techniques to access *menus* from the *menu bar* and to issue *commands* from the menus. If you click the right mouse button while pointing at certain areas of the display, a *shortcut menu* is displayed. When you issue some commands, a *dialog box* is displayed.

- When you use any program, you save your work on a *hard disk* or *diskette* in files that are organized in *folders*.

- The Open and Save As commands work similarly for all programs that were designed to run under Windows 95 and NT 4.

- You can use dialog boxes like Open and Save As to manage folders and files. You can also use the Windows Explorer to manage folders and files.

- You can "undelete" files that you've deleted from a hard drive on your PC by restoring them from the Recycle Bin.

- You can use the Find command in the Start menu to search an entire drive for folders and files.

Chapter 2

Eleven more Windows skills and the Help feature

This chapter starts by presenting eleven skills that can help you work more effectively with Windows 95 or NT 4. Right now, you may feel that you don't need any of these extra skills, but sooner or later you'll find the need for one or more of them. Then, you can go directly to the skill that you need.

This chapter ends by showing you how to use the standard Help feature for Windows 95 and NT 4. This feature is useful when you need to do a Windows function that isn't presented in this book. If you're like most Windows users, though, you may never find the need for other functions.

Eleven more Windows skills 36
How to use shortcuts on your desktop 36
How to add shortcuts to your desktop 37
How to add shortcuts to the top of the Start menu 38
How to organize your Start menu 39
How to control the view in folder windows 40
How to work with the Control Panel 41
How to work with local drives 42
How to work with network drives 43
How to share local files and printers 44
How to work with printers 45
How to manage the print queue 46

When and how to get online help 47
How to use the Help Topics dialog box 47
How to work with a Help topic 48
How to get help from a dialog box 49

Perspective
Summary

Eleven more Windows skills

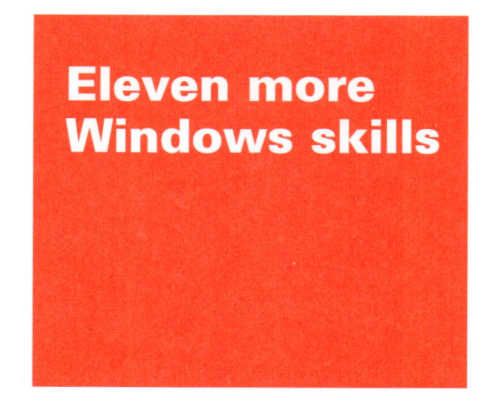

The eleven skills that are presented here are some of the most useful Windows 95 and NT skills. Even if you don't need them right now, you should be aware of them.

Incidentally, you can do many of the skills that follow in more than one way. For instance, you can work with the files in a folder from either the Explorer or from a folder window. The methods that are illustrated are just the ones that we prefer.

How to use shortcuts on your desktop

Figure 2-1 shows a desktop that contains shortcuts for programs, folders, files, and a printer. As you can see from this figure, you can use shortcuts to start programs and documents, to explore folders, and to work with printers. Usually, you double-click on a shortcut to start it, but sometimes you'll want to right-click a shortcut to access a context-sensitive menu.

When you have shortcuts on your desktop, you need to be able to view them before you can use them. Once you start a program and maximize its window, for example, you won't be able to see the desktop. In that case, you need to minimize the program window before you can access shortcuts from your desktop.

When you work with shortcuts, keep in mind that they only point to the folders and files they represent. As a

A desktop that contains shortcuts to programs, folders, files, and a printer

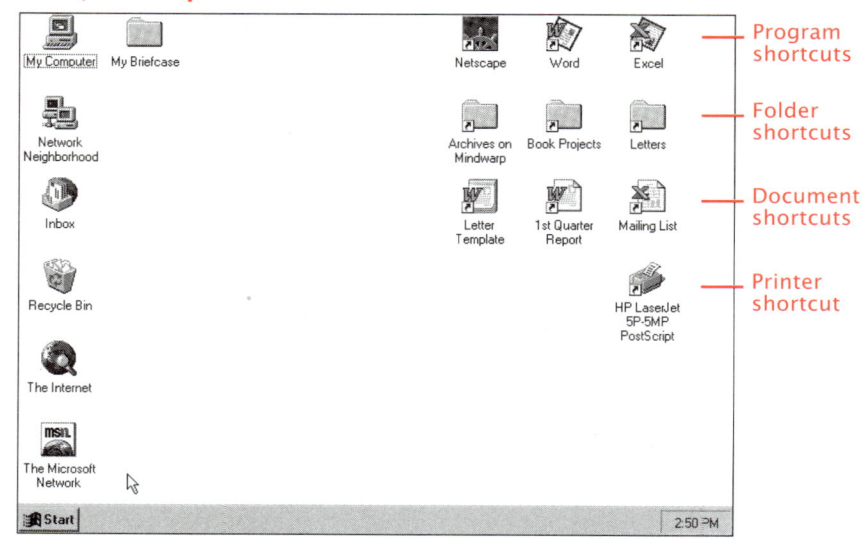

How to use shortcuts

- To start a program, double-click on the shortcut for the program.
- To open a document and its parent program, double-click on the shortcut for the document.
- To explore the contents of a folder, double-click on the shortcut for the folder to open its folder window.
- To print a document, drag its shortcut to the printer shortcut and drop it.
- If open windows prevent you from seeing the shortcut you want to use, right-click on the taskbar and select the Minimize All Windows command from the shortcut menu.

How to organize shortcuts

- To align all shortcuts and other icons on your desktop, right-click on a blank area on the desktop and select the Line Up Icons command from the shortcut menu. Or, to automatically keep the icons aligned, select Arrange Icons from the shortcut menu and then select Auto Arrange from its submenu.
- To move or copy a shortcut, use the standard Cut, Copy, and Paste commands as described in chapter 1.
- To delete a shortcut, drag it to the Recycle Bin, or click on the shortcut to highlight it and press the Delete key.
- To rename a shortcut, right-click on the shortcut to highlight it and select Rename from the shortcut menu. Then, type a new name and press Enter.

Note

- All shortcuts have a shortcut icon ( ) in their lower left corner that identifies them as shortcuts.

Figure 2-1 How to use shortcuts on your desktop

result, you can move, copy, delete, or rename a shortcut without affecting the folder or file the shortcut points to.

How to add shortcuts to your desktop

You can create a shortcut for just about any type of Windows object, including folders and files on network drives. In general, if you use a resource often, you should consider creating a shortcut for it, especially if the resource is hard to access. Then, you won't waste time navigating through menus and dialog boxes to get to the resources you need.

Figure 2-2 shows how to create a shortcut on your desktop. Although you'll usually want to create shortcuts on your desktop as shown in the figure, you can create shortcuts in any folder on your system. To do that, just follow the procedure shown in figure 2-2, but drag the object to the folder you want. If you accidentally create a shortcut in the wrong location, you can delete it or move it as described in figure 2-1.

How to create a shortcut

1. Close or minimize all open windows so the desktop is displayed.
2. Start the Explorer and navigate through it until the object you want is displayed.
3. If necessary, click on the Restore button for the Explorer so you can see the Explorer and the desktop as shown below. To do this, you may need to move or resize the Explorer window.
4. Right-drag the object you want from the Explorer to the desktop. When you do, you'll get a shortcut menu like this:

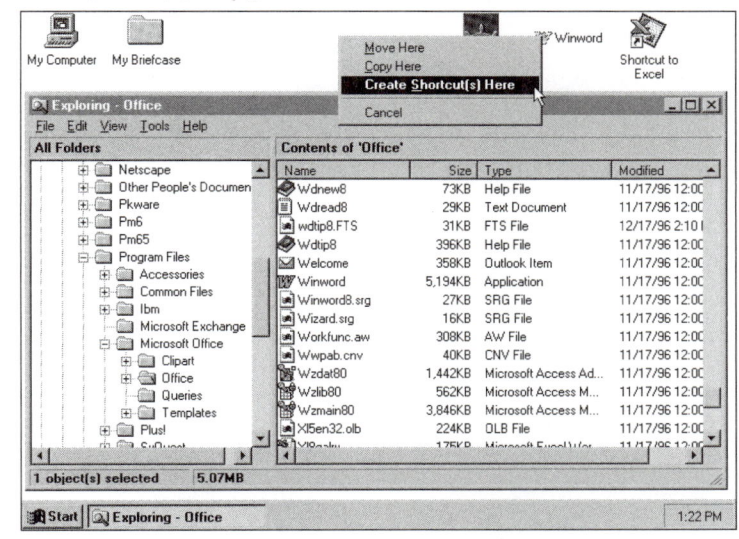

5. Select the Create Shortcut Here command and the shortcut is created.

Notes

- You can also create a shortcut for an application program by left-dragging it to the desktop. In that case, the shortcut menu shown above isn't displayed.
- On some types of networks, you can create shortcuts to folders on networked drives. So, if you spend a lot of time navigating to a folder on a networked drive, try creating a shortcut for it.
- Besides creating a shortcut for a document, you can create a shortcut for a template that you use for starting other documents.

Warning

- If you left-drag a folder or file from the Explorer to the desktop, the folder or file is actually moved to the desktop. As a result, you won't be able to find it in its earlier Explorer location. Instead, you will find it subordinate to the Desktop at the top of the Explorer's folder structure. Since that usually isn't what you want, be sure to right-drag a folder or file when you want to create a shortcut for it.

Figure 2-2   How to add shortcuts to your desktop

How to add shortcuts to the top of the Start menu

Figure 2-3 shows how to add a shortcut to the top of the Start menu. The first screen shows what a typical Start menu will look like when one shortcut is added. The second screen shows what the Start menu will look like with small icons and six shortcuts.

The advantage of putting shortcuts at the top of the Start menu is that they are always available to you regardless of how many windows you have open. As a result, you can always access the shortcuts at the top of the Start menu with just two clicks. The disadvantage is that the Start menu can only hold about twelve shortcuts…and that's if you're using small icons. So when you add shortcuts to the top of the Start menu, you should make sure they're the ones you'll be using most of the time.

A Start menu with one shortcut and large icons

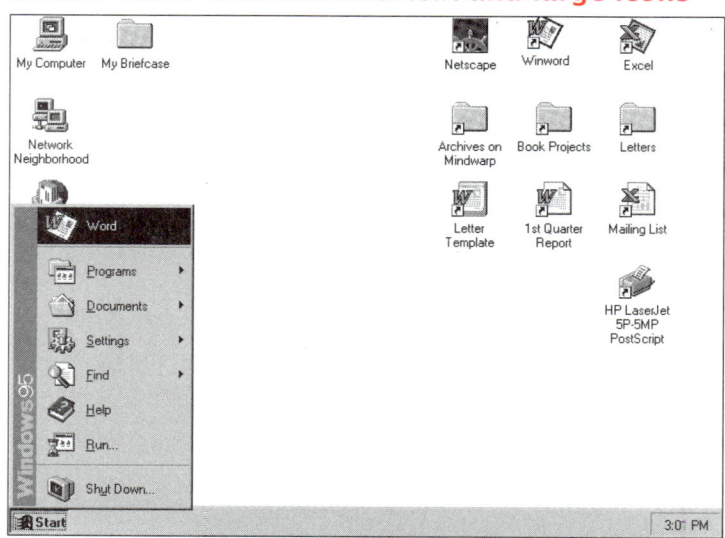

A Start menu with 6 shortcuts and small icons

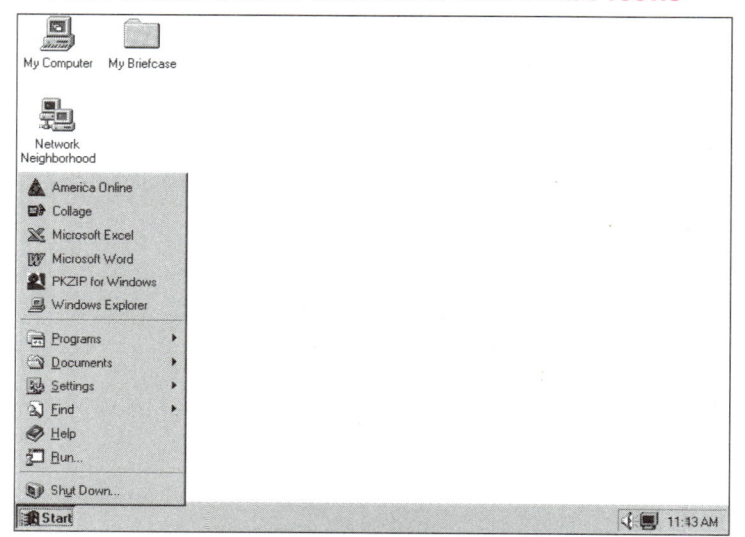

How to add a shortcut to the top of the Start menu

- If you have already created a shortcut on the desktop, just drag it to the Start button and release it. Windows then creates a copy of the shortcut and adds it to the Start menu.
- If you haven't created a shortcut, start the Explorer and drag the object that you want to the Start button.

How to remove shortcuts

- Use the procedures shown in figure 2-4 to delete or move the shortcut from the top of the Start menu.

How to show small icons in the Start menu

- Right-click on a blank area of the taskbar, select the Properties command from the shortcut menu, and select the Show Small Icons in Start Menu option in the Taskbar Options tab.

Figure 2-3 How to add shortcuts to the top of the Start menu

Chapter 2   Eleven more skills and the Help feature   39

How to organize your Start menu

If your computer has a lot of programs installed on it, it's likely that the Program submenu of the Start menu is poorly organized. That can make it hard for you to find the program you want, and it can create many layers of menus for you to navigate.

Figure 2-4 shows how to work with the Programs menu and the top of the Start menu. First, it shows how to add a program to either of these menus. Then, it shows how to use the Explorer to organize the items on these menus. The main concept here is that each folder in the Explorer window represents a menu and each item in a folder represents a menu item.

Although you can also use the Remove button to remove items, the Advanced option gives you more options and is usually faster for anyone who is proficient with the Explorer.

Additional Information

✓ The StartUp folder shown in the Explorer window above is a special folder. If you put a shortcut in this folder, Windows 95 will automatically launch the program each time you start your PC.

✓ Some programs automatically install themselves into the StartUp folder.

The Taskbar Properties dialog box

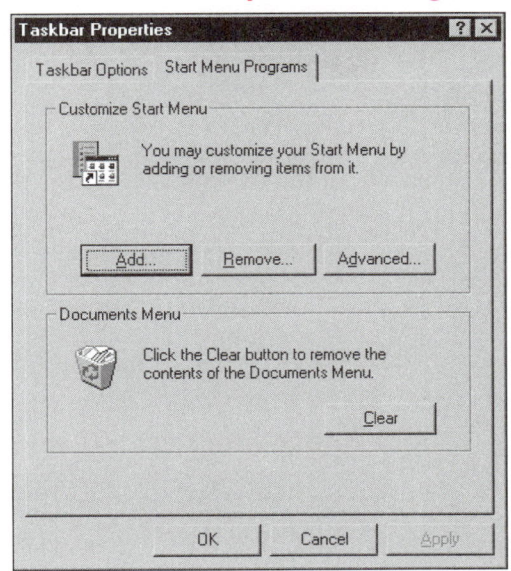

The Explorer window you get when you click on the Advanced button

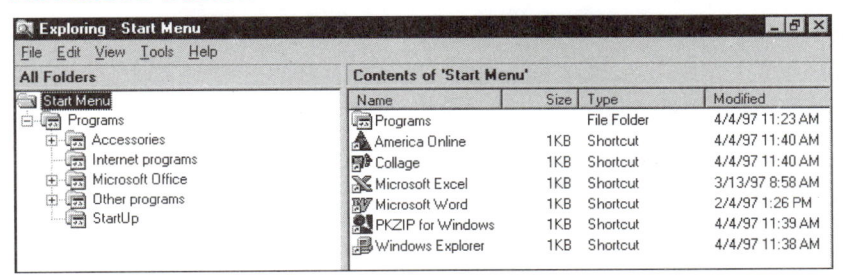

How to add a program to the Start menu

1. Right-click on a blank area on the taskbar, select the Properties command, and click on the Start Menu Programs tab to access a dialog box like the one shown above.
2. Click on the Add button.
3. Follow the instructions in the dialog boxes that follow to create a shortcut for the program and add it to one of the menus.

How to organize your Start menu

1. Right-click on a blank area on the taskbar, select the Properties command, and click on the Start Menu Programs tab to access a dialog box like the one shown above.
2. Click on the Advanced button to access an Explorer window like the one shown above.
3. Use the Explorer techniques you learned in chapter 1 to organize the folders and the shortcuts within the folders. Usually, you'll only need to move folders and files.

Figure 2-4   How to organize your Start menu

How to control the view in folder windows

Figure 2-5 shows you how to control the view in a folder window. In general, when a folder doesn't contain many items, the Large Icons view can help to reduce eyestrain. However, when a folder contains too many icons to fit in the window, you'll want to use one of the other three views (Small Icons, List, or Details) to reduce the amount of scrolling you have to do to find the item you want.

When you work with folder windows, you'll occasionally need to sort items by name, type, size, or date. This can make it easier to locate and select the folders and files you need. For example, if you're running out of disk space and you want to see what files are taking up the most disk space, you can sort by size. Or, if you want to copy the last four files you worked on to another folder, you can sort by date.

You can think of the Windows Explorer as a special kind of folder window. In particular, the View menu for the Explorer is the same as the View menu shown in figure 2-5. As a result, you can use the techniques described in this figure to work with the Explorer.

A folder window with large icons

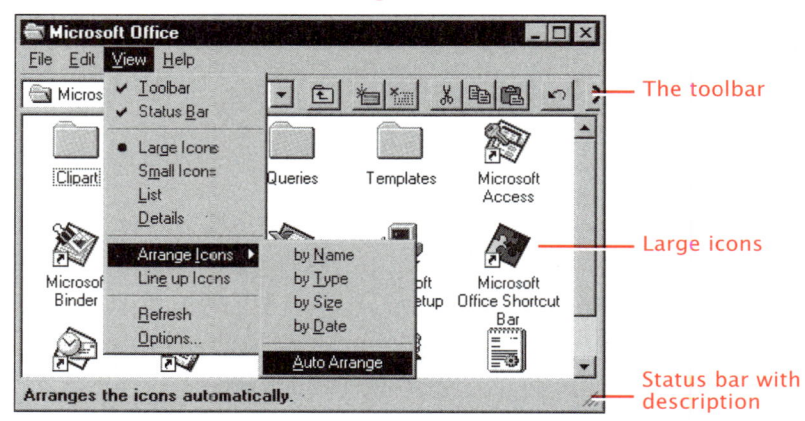

A folder window with small icons

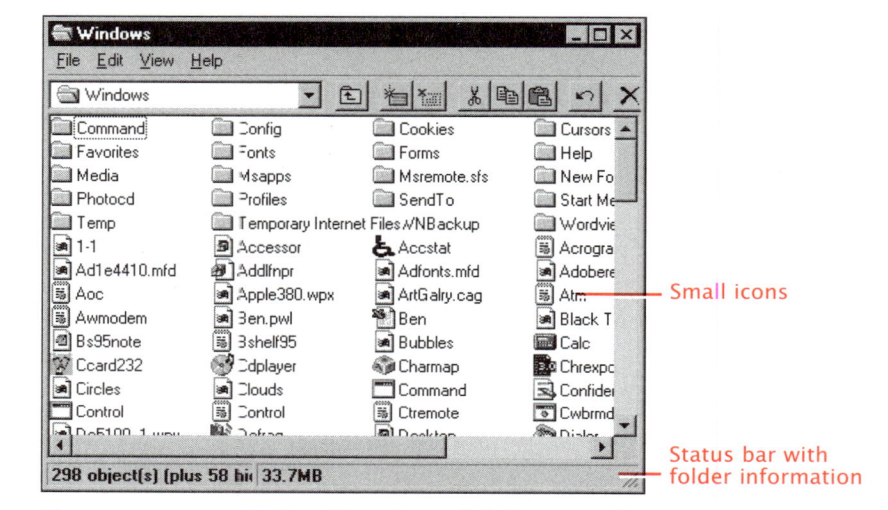

How to control the view in a folder window

- To display the toolbar or the status bar, select the Toolbar or Status Bar commands as shown above. To hide the toolbar or the status bar, deselect the Toolbar or Status Bar commands.

- To switch views, select the Large Icons, Small Icons, List, or Details command from the View menu. Or, click on one of the four toolbar buttons that show when the window is maximized (not shown above).

- To sort the icons in a window by name, type, size, or date, select the appropriate command from the Arrange Icons submenu shown above. If you're using the Details view, you can sort the files in a window by name, type, size, or date by clicking on the heading for the column and by clicking a second time to reverse the sort sequence.

- To have Windows automatically arrange the icons for you, select the Auto Arrange command shown above.

- If you make a change that doesn't show up in a folder window, try selecting the Refresh command from the View menu.

How to control the view in the Explorer window

- You can use the same techniques shown above to control the view in the right pane of the Explorer window.

Figure 2-5   How to control the view in folder windows

Chapter 2 Eleven more skills and the Help feature 41

How to work with the Control Panel

Figure 2-6 summarizes the Control Panel items that are likely to be available on your PC. Since Windows usually does a good job of setting up your system, you usually won't need to use these icons to adjust your system settings. However, there are times when you need to use the Control Panel to get your PC to work the way you want it to.

When you work with the Control Panel, you start by double-clicking on the items. When you do, you may get a single dialog box that contains several tabs. Or, you may get a wizard that steps you through a process. Either way, the dialog boxes are usually easy to understand. If you don't understand them, you can try using the Question Mark button that's described in figure 2-14. Or you can try using the Help Topics dialog box described later in this chapter.

The Control Panel folder

How to access the Control Panel

- Click on the Start button, point to the Settings command to display its submenu, and select the Control Panel command. When you do, you'll get a dialog box like the one shown above.

A summary of ten standard items in the Control Panel

Option	Function
Date/Time	Set your PC's internal clock
Mouse	Adjust the sensitivity of the mouse
Keyboard	Adjust the sensitivity of the keyboard
Display	Control the appearance of Windows on your monitor
Fonts shortcut	View, add, and remove fonts
Add/Remove Programs	Install and uninstall application programs and Windows components
Add New Hardware	Add new hardware to your system
Passwords	Control the passwords you use to log on to Windows and turn the User Profile feature on and off
Network	Configure network hardware and software
System	Change advanced settings that control how your system works

Note

- You can access the same dialog box as the Date/Time icon by double-clicking on the clock that's displayed on the right side of the taskbar.

Figure 2-6 How to work with the Control Panel

How to work with local drives

In chapter 1, you learned that the My Computer folder contains all the *local drives* that are available to your computer. Figure 2-7 shows you how to work with the local drives that are available to your computer. In particular, it focuses on how to work with diskettes and diskette drives.

Keep in mind that you can *map a network drive* to your computer as shown in figure 2-8. Then, the network drive appears in the My Computer folder and is associated with a letter. In that case, you can work with the network drive much as if it were a local drive.

To *format* a diskette is to prepare it so it can store information. When you format a diskette, all files on the diskette are erased. Most modern computer systems use 3.5-inch diskettes that are formatted to store 1.44 megabytes of data, so that's what you'll usually want to do.

Occasionally, you may want to make a copy of an entire diskette. Since most PCs only have one diskette drive, you usually specify the same drive in the Copy From and Copy To boxes as shown in figure 2-7.

The shortcut menu that's displayed when you right-click on the diskette drive for a computer

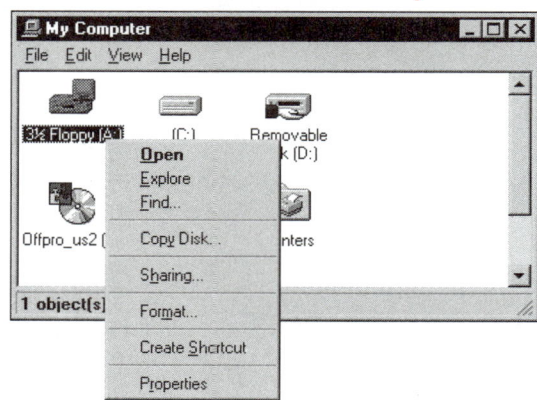

How to check the amount of free space on a drive

- Right-click on the drive and select the Properties command. When you do, you'll get a dialog box that tells you the amount of free and used space on the drive.

How to format a diskette

1. Insert the diskette into the drive.
2. Access the My Computer folder, right-click on the diskette drive, and select the Format command. When you do, you'll get a Format dialog box that lets you set a variety of options including the capacity of the diskette and whether you want to do a quick format or a full format.
3. By default, the Format dialog box is set to do a quick format on your primary diskette drive. If that's what you want, click on the Start button to begin formatting. Otherwise, change the options before you click on the Start button.

How to make a copy of an entire diskette

1. Insert the diskette you want to make a copy of into the diskette drive.
2. Right-click on the diskette drive and select the Copy Disk command. When you do, you'll get a dialog box like this:

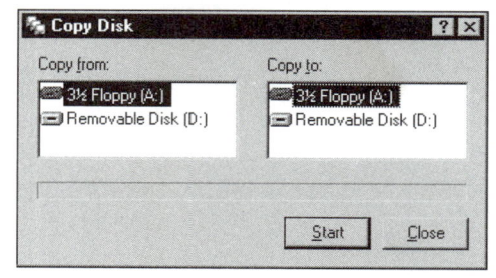

3. Select the drives you want to use in the Copy From and Copy To boxes.
4. Click on the Start button and follow the instructions that are displayed.

Note

- The commands in the shortcut menu vary depending on the type of drive. Some CD-ROM drives and other types of removable drives include Eject and Play commands.

Figure 2-7   How to work with local drives

How to work with network drives

If you use Microsoft's networking software, you can use the Network Neighborhood to access the folders and files on other computers on the network. In general, you navigate through the networked computers, folders, and files in much the same way that you navigate through folders and files on your local drives. And you can move and copy files between local and networked drives in the same way too.

When you set up a network, you assign each computer to a *workgroup*. Workgroups provide a way to group computers that are used to perform similar functions. The system shown in figure 2-8, for example, contains three workgroups. Notice that all of the computers in the same workgroup as your computer appear directly under the Network Neighborhood so they're easy to get to.

If your network includes one or more *servers*, they're listed under the name of the *domain* that contains them. Servers can perform a variety of functions, but they're used most often to store files or control printers that can be accessed by anyone on the network.

To make it easier to access a drive or folder on another computer on the network, you can map it to your computer as described in figure 2-8. When you map a network resource, it appears as another drive in your My Computer folder. Then, you can access it just as you would any other drive on your local computer.

If you try to access a network resource that you're not authorized to use, Windows will display a message telling you that your access is denied. To obtain access to this resource, you may need to contact your network administrator.

The Network Neighborhood as viewed by the Explorer

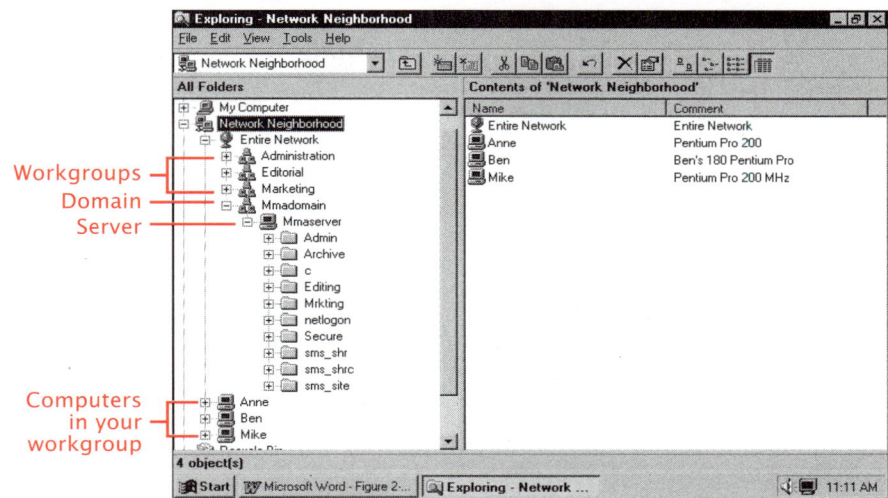

How network computers are grouped

- A computer must be either a member of a *workgroup* or a *domain*. Workgroups usually consist of desktop computers that perform related functions. A domain always contains at least one *server* that controls the domain and may contain other servers and desktop computers.

How to map a network drive or folder to your computer

1. Start the Explorer and navigate to the drive or folder in the Network Neighborhood that you want to map.
2. Right-click on the drive or folder and select the Map Network Drive command to display this dialog box:
3. Select the letter you want to map the drive to from the Drive list, select the Reconnect At Logon option, and click on the OK button.

How to disconnect a mapped drive

- Locate the drive in the My Computer folder, right-click on it, and select the Disconnect command from the resulting menu.

Note

- If the Map Network Drive command isn't available, you can't map the selected folder. In that case, try mapping its parent folder.

Figure 2-8 **How to work with network drives**

How to share local files and printers

If you have a *file server* connected to your network, you'll probably use it to store files that need to be accessed by other users. And if you have a *print server* connected to your network, anyone on the network can print to the printers that it controls. If you don't have a file or print server on the network, though, or even if you do, you may want to share files and printers on your local computer so that others can access them. Figure 2-9 shows you how.

Before you can share resources on your system, you have to activate sharing. You can activate file sharing, print sharing, or both. When you activate either type of sharing, the name of your computer appears in the Network Neighborhood as shown in figure 2-8.

After you activate sharing, you need to tell Windows what drives, folders, and printers you want to share. For each resource, you specify the name you want Windows to use to identify the resource. You can also specify a password for the resource. Then, only those users that know the password can access the resource. For a drive or folder, you also specify the type of access you want other users to have to the resource. The default is read-only, but you can also give full access to the files.

Additional information

✓ The name that's displayed for a computer in the Network Neighborhood is taken from the Identification tab of the Network dialog box. To change this name, access the control panel, double-click on the Network icon, click on the Identification tab and type a new name. You can also change the workgroup that your computer belongs to from this dialog box.

How to activate file and print sharing

1. Access the control panel, double-click on the Network icon, and click on the File and Print Sharing button to display this dialog box:

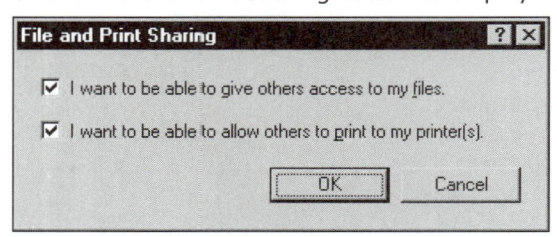

2. Select the appropriate options to give other network users access to files and printers on your computer. Click on the OK button, then restart your computer when prompted so the settings take effect.

How to share files on your local computer

1. Use the Explorer to find the drive or folder that contains the files you want to share. Then, right-click on it and select the Sharing command to display this dialog box:

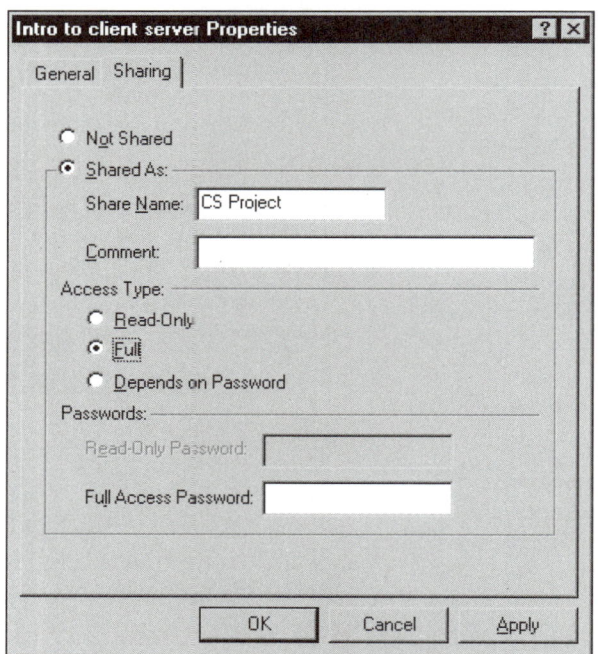

2. Click on the Shared As option, enter the name you want to use for the shared drive or folder in the Share Name text box, choose the type of access you want to allow from the Access Type group, and enter a password if appropriate.

3. Click on the OK button and the icon for the drive or folder will change to include a hand that indicates that it's shared.

How to share a printer on your local computer

- Use the same procedure as for sharing files. The only difference is that you don't specify an access type for a printer.

Figure 2-9   How to share local files and printers

Chapter 2   Eleven more skills and the Help feature   45

How to work with printers

A *local printer* is a printer that's attached directly to your PC. A *network printer* is a printer that's available to you through your network. Before you can use a printer, the correct *print driver* must be installed on your system. A print driver is the piece of software that controls how your computer and printer interact.

When you use Windows 95 and NT 4, the Printers folder stores the print drivers for all local and network printers that are installed on your system. You can access this folder from the Settings command on the Start menu.

Figure 2-10 shows how to work with the printers that are installed on your system. If you have access to more than one printer, you'll want to make sure the printer you use most often is set as the *default printer*. In addition, you may want to create a shortcut for the printers you use most often, and you may need to install a print driver for a local printer or a network printer.

The shortcut menu that's displayed when you right-click on a printer in the Printers folder

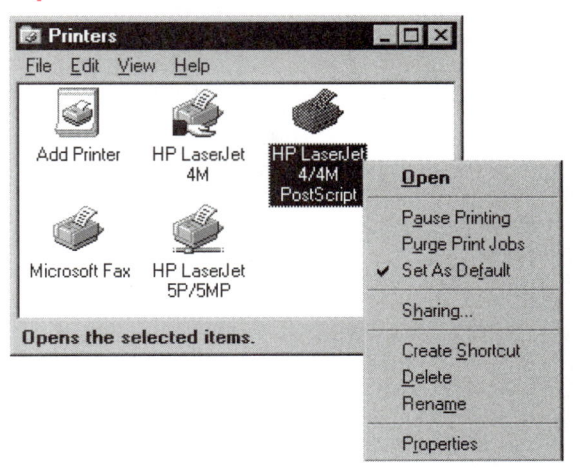

How to access the Printers folder

- Click on the Start button, point to Settings, and select the Printers command.

How to set the default printer

- Right-click on the printer, and select the Set As Default command so it has a check mark next to it as shown above.

How to add a print driver to your system

1. Double-click on the Add Printer icon to access the Add Printer Wizard.
2. Follow the Wizard's instructions.

How to share a printer on your local computer

1. Right-click on the printer and select the Sharing command. This is a second way to access the Properties dialog box for the printer. The first way is from the Explorer as summarized in figure 2-9.
2. Click on the Shared As option and complete the dialog box as summarized in figure 2-9. When you're through, the printer icon includes a hand to indicate that it's shared as shown by the second icon in the folder window above.

Figure 2-10   How to work with printers

How to manage the print queue

When you print a document, Windows 95 and NT 4 create a temporary file known as a *print job* and send the print job to the printer's *print queue*. A print queue is simply a list of the jobs that are waiting to be printed. Since the print queue runs in the background, you can usually continue working while your documents are printing.

Suppose, however, that you start the printing of a document and then realize that there's an error in the document you just sent to the printer. In that case, you can cancel the print job as shown in figure 2-11.

A print queue with four print jobs

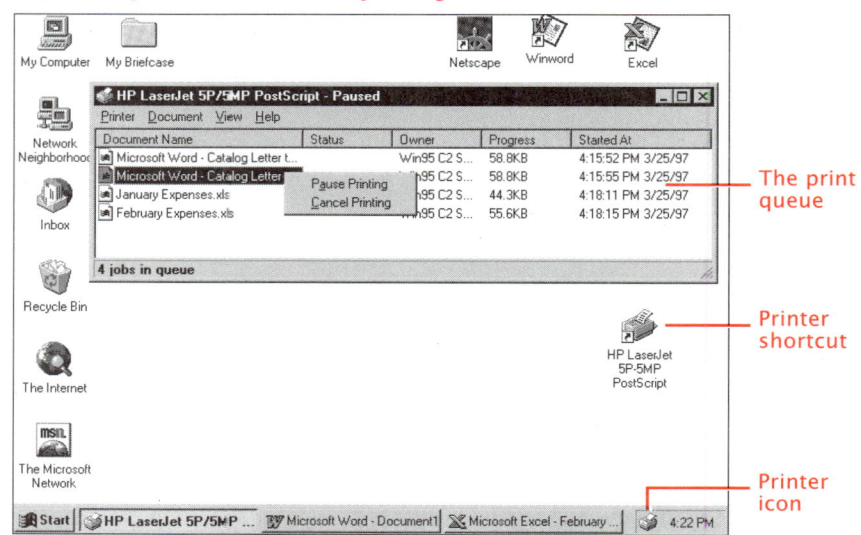

Two ways to access the print queue

- Double-click on the printer icon in the notification area of the taskbar.
- If you have a shortcut for the printer on your desktop, double-click on it.

How to cancel a print job

- Right-click on the print job and select the Cancel command from the shortcut menu.

How to pause a print job

- Right-click on the print job and select the Pause Printing command from the shortcut menu. To restart printing, right-click on the paused job and deselect the Pause Printing command.

Two ways to cancel or pause all print jobs

- Access the print queue, and select the Purge Print Jobs or Pause Printing command from the Printer menu.
- If you have a shortcut for the printer on your desktop, right-click on the shortcut and select the Purge Print Jobs or Pause Printing command from the shortcut menu.

Notes

- When a print job is in a print queue for a network printer, you may or may not have control over it. That depends on the network you're using and how that network is set up. Most likely, you'll be able to cancel and pause jobs that you send to the queue, but you won't be able to affect jobs that other people have sent to the queue.
- The examples above show the command names that are used with Windows 95. If you're using Windows NT 4, you may notice that the command names are slightly different.

Figure 2-11 How to manage the print queue

When and how to get online help

If you experiment with the Help feature for Windows, you'll see that it provides a wide variety of information. This information can be useful when you need to do a function that isn't included in this book.

How to use the Help Topics dialog box

The Help Topics dialog box is a standard dialog box for Windows 95 and NT 4 and for all programs that were designed to run under Windows 95 and NT 4. To get help information about Windows, just select the Help command from the Start menu.

As you can see in figure 2-12, the Help Topics dialog box contains three tabs: Contents, Index, and Find. All three tabs lead to help information like the information shown in Figure 2-13. However, each tab provides a unique way to search for the information that you need.

The bottom of figure 2-12 shows how to use all three tabs of the Help Topics dialog box. If you experiment with them, you'll see that they're all easy to use. When you use the Contents tab, you'll see that it breaks the Help topics down into broad subjects that you can *collapse* or *expand* by double-clicking on them. When you work with the Index and Find tabs, you'll see that they let you search for a topic by typing text into a text box.

How to access the Help Topics dialog box
- To get information about Windows 95 or NT 4, select the Help command from the Start menu.

The Contents tab of the Help Topics dialog box

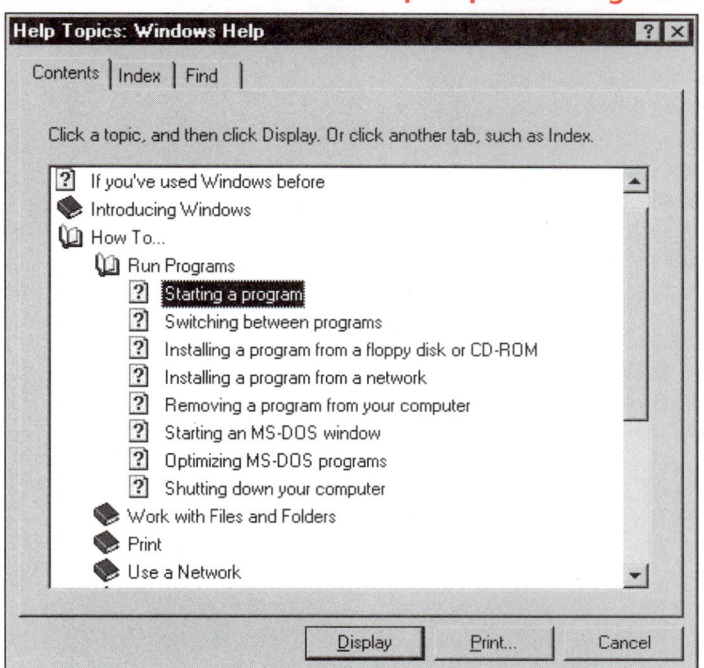

How to use the Contents tab
- To display the topics available for a particular subject, double-click on the subject. Or, click on the subject and then click on the Open button.
- To hide the topics for a subject, double-click on the subject. Or, click on the subject and then click on the Close button.
- To display Help information for a topic, double-click on the topic. Or, click on the topic and then click on the Display button.

How to use the Index tab
- Type a word or phrase in the text box at the top of the dialog box. Then, double-click on the index entry you want.

How to use the Find tab
- Type a word or phrase in the text box at the top of the dialog box. If necessary, click on a word in the second box to limit the number of topics that are displayed. Then, double-click on the topic you want.
- The first time you access the Find tab, you'll get a wizard that helps you create a database that the Find tab needs in order to work.

How to print Help information
- To print the Help information for a topic, click on the topic. Then, click on the Print button and respond to the resulting Print dialog box.

Figure 2-12 How to use the Help Topics dialog box

How to work with a Help topic

Figure 2-13 shows an example of a Help topic. Notice that the topic is displayed in its own window. By default, this window only takes up about a third of the screen and always remains on top of the other windows. In this figure, for example, you can see that the Help window is on top of the Explorer window even though the Explorer window is the active window. That makes it easy to follow the step-by-step instructions in a Help window.

Since the Help information is displayed in a window, you can use standard techniques for working with windows to minimize, maximize, restore, close, move, and size the window. And you can use standard techniques to switch between the Help window and other windows.

As you work with the Help feature, you'll find that some Help topics do more than just display information. For instance, some Help topics provide a visual overview of a feature. Others lead you step by step through a procedure. And still others provide buttons, icons, and highlighted words that lead you to additional information.

The Help topic in Figure 2-13 illustrates two of these special features. If you click on the underlined word, "taskbar," near the middle of the Help topic, a definition of that word is displayed. And if you click on the Related Topics button at the bottom of the topic, a dialog box is displayed that lets you choose from some related topics. If you spend a few minutes experimenting with these special features, you shouldn't have any trouble figuring out how they work.

A Windows Help topic displayed on top of the Explorer

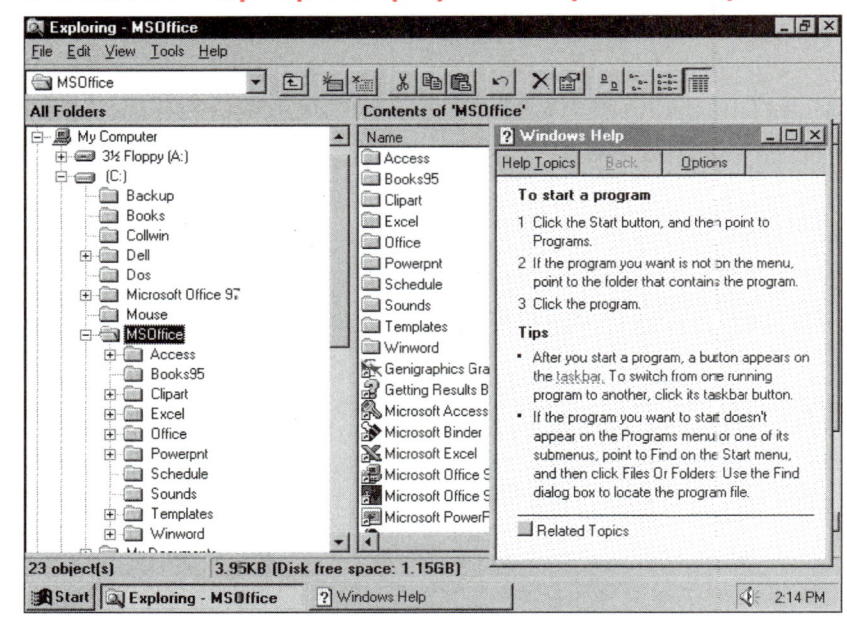

Operation

- To return to the Help Topics dialog box, click on the Help Topics button.
- To return to the last Help topic you viewed, click on the Back button.
- To print the topic, click on the Options button, select the Print Topics command, and respond to the resulting Print dialog box. You can also use the Options button to copy the current topic into a word processor, to change the font size and color of the topic, and to control how the Help window behaves.

Notes

- A Help topic is displayed in its own program window. By default, this window is displayed on the right side of the screen and stays on top of any other programs that are running. All standard techniques for moving and sizing windows apply to this window as do all standard techniques for switching between programs.
- Some Help topics contain buttons, icons, and underlined words that you can click on to get other help information.

Figure 2-13 How to work with a Help topic

How to get help from a dialog box

Sometimes you'll just want some information about one of the controls on a dialog box. Then, you don't need to access the Help Topics dialog box. Instead, you can use the techniques shown in Figure 2-14. In some cases, all you need to do is point at the control and click the right mouse button. In other cases, however, you'll need to use the Question Mark button in the title bar of the dialog box.

A dialog box with Help information displayed

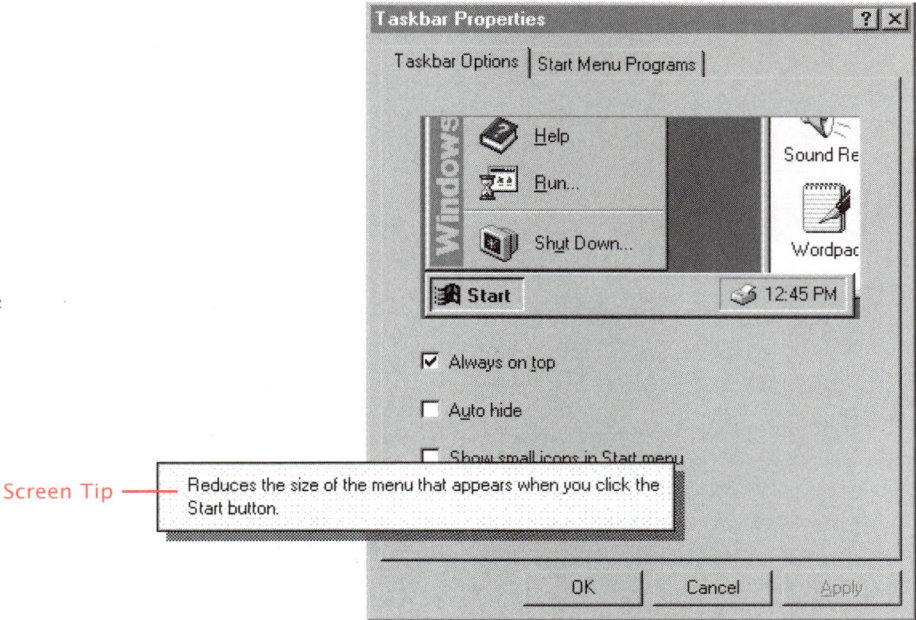

Screen Tip

How to use the Question Mark button to get help from a dialog box

1. Click on the Question Mark button in the upper right corner of the dialog box. Then, a question mark is added to your mouse pointer.
2. Click on the dialog box control that you want more information about. A ScreenTip is displayed that provides a brief explanation of the control.
3. To close the ScreenTip, click on it.

Other ways to get help from a dialog box

- You can access some ScreenTips just by right-clicking on the dialog box control. If the What's This command appears when you do that, click on the command to display the ScreenTip.
- To display ScreenTips using keyboard techniques, move the focus to the control you want Help information on and press F1. To close the ScreenTip, press the Esc key.

Figure 2-14 How to get help from a dialog box

Perspective

This chapter has presented eleven more Windows skills that you should at least be aware of. Once you get used to Windows 95 or NT, you're probably going to want to use one or more of these skills because they can help you work more efficiently.

Summary

- You can create *shortcuts* for programs, folders, files, and printers.
- You can add shortcuts to your desktop or to the top of the Start menu.
- You can use the Start Menu Programs tab of the Taskbar Properties dialog box to organize the items that are shown at the top of the Start menu and all items that are shown on the Programs menu and its submenus.
- You can use the View menu of a folder window to control how the items within the folder are displayed.
- You can use the Control Panel to control how your computer looks and behaves.
- The My Computer folder displays all *local drives* or drives that are attached to your computer. Before you can use a *diskette* in a *diskette drive*, you need to *format* it so it can store information.
- The Network Neighborhood folder displays all *network drives* that are available to your computer. You can *map* a network drive so that it appears in the My Computer folder and behaves much like a local drive.
- To share files and printers on your local computer so others can access them, you first activate sharing. Then, you tell Windows what drives, folders, or printers you want to share.
- You can use the Printers folder to work with *local printers* (printers that are directly attached to your computer) and *network printers* (printers that are available through a network). You'll want to use this folder to set the printer you use most often as the *default printer*.
- When you print a document, a *print job* is sent to a list of jobs known as the *print queue*. Then, the list of jobs are sent to the printer. You can double-click on the *printer icon* in the taskbar to manage the print queue.
- You can use the standard Help Topics dialog box to get Help information about Windows 95 and NT 4.
- You can use the Question Mark button to get Help information about a control on a dialog box.

Index

A

Adding
    to Program submenu, 39
    to Start menu, 38, 39
Aligning icons, 36, 40
Alt+Tab switching, 10
Application window, 8-11
Arranging icons, 36, 40
Automatic program startup, 39

C

Cancelling a print job, 46
CD-ROM drive, 22, 42
Check box, 18
Clicking the mouse, 4
Clock, 3, 41
Close button, 11, 18, 20
Closing a window, 11
Collapsing
    folder, 29
    Help subjects, 47
Command, 16
Command button, 18
Context sensitive menu, 17
Control menu and icon, 11
Control Panel, 2, 4, 41, 44
Converting file formats, 26
Copying
    diskette, 42
    file or folder, 28-29
    Help information, 48
    shortcut, 36
Creating
    folder, 28-29
    shortcut, 37
Current folder, 23

D

Date/Time setting, 41
Default printer, 45
Deleting
    file or folder, 28-29
    shortcut, 36, 37
Desktop, 3
Dialog box, 18-20
Directory (Windows 3.1), 22

Disk drive, 22, 42
    local, 42
    mapping, 22-23
    network, 42
    selecting, 25
Diskette drive, 22, 42
Display settings, 41
Displaying a shortcut menu, 17
Document file, 23
Document shortcut, 36-38
Document window, 8-9
    scrolling, 13
Domain, 2, 43
DOS, 6
Double-clicking the mouse, 4
Dragging the mouse, 4
Drive, *see Disk drive*
Drive icon, 9

E

Emptying the Recycle Bin, 30
Exit command (File menu), 20
Exiting
    from an application, 11, 20
    from Windows, 6
Expanding
    folder, 29
    Help subjects, 47
Explorer, 22, 23, 29, 40, 44
Extension, 23, 26, 27

F

File, 22, 24, 26, 27, 28-29, 30, 44
File extension, 23, 26, 27
File icon, 9
File name, 23, 27
File server, 43, 44
Focus, 19
Folder, 22, 23, 25, 28-29, 30, 36, 44
Folder icon, 9
Folder shortcut, 36-38
Folder window, 8, 40
Fonts, 41
Formatting a diskette, 42

H

Hard disk, 22
Help information, 47-49
Help menu, 47
Horizontal scroll bar, 13

I

Icon, 3, 9, 36, 38, 40

K

Keyboard sensitivity, 41

L

List box, 18
Local drive, 42
Local file, 44
Local printer, 44, 45
Logging on, 2
Logo screen, 2

M

Mapping a disk drive, 22-23, 43
Maximizing a window, 11-12
Menu, 5, 9, 16
Microsoft Office Shortcut Bar, 3, 9
Microsoft networking, 43
Minimizing a window, 11-12
Minimizing all windows, 11, 36
Mouse actions, 4
Mouse pointer, 4
Mouse sensitivity, 41
Moving
    file or folder, 28-29
    shortcut, 36, 37
    window, 12
MS-DOS, 6
My Computer, 22

N

Network, 22, 41
Network Neighborhood, 22, 25, 43, 44
Network printer, 45
Network server, 43
Notification area, 3

O

Open command (File menu), 24
Opening
    file, 22
    program, 36
    window, 9, 36
Option button, 18
Options command (Tools menu), 20

Index

Organizing
    Program submenu, 39
    shortcuts, 36
    Start menu, 39

P

Pane, 22
Pausing a printer, 46
Password, 2, 41
Pointing the mouse, 4
Print driver, 45
Print job, 46
Print queue, 46
Printer, 36, 44, 45
Printer shortcut, 36-38
Printing
    document, 36
    Help information, 47, 48
Program, 8
    exiting, 11, 20
    starting, 5, 9, 29, 36, 38, 39
Program file, 23
Program menu, 39
Program shortcut, 36-38
Program window, 8-11

Q

Question Mark button, 41

R

Rebooting the PC, 6
Recycle Bin, 30
Refresh command, 40
Removing shortcut from Start menu, 38
Renaming
    file or folder, 28-29
    shortcut, 36
Restarting the PC, 6
Restoring
    file or folder, 30
    window, 11-12
Right-clicking the mouse, 4
Right-dragging the mouse, 4

S

Save As command (File menu), 27
Saving a file, 27
ScreenTip, 49
Scroll arrow, 13
Scroll bar, 13
Scroll box, 13
Scrolling, 13
Selecting
    disk drive, 25
    file, 26
    folder, 25
Server, 43, 44
Sharing, 44
Shortcut, 36-38
Shortcut bar, 3
Shortcut icon, 3, 9
Shortcut key, 16
Shortcut menu, 17
Shutting down the PC, 6
Sizing a window, 12
Slide bar, 18
Sorting icons or files, 40
Spin box, 18
Start button, 3
Start menu, 5, 9, 38-39, 47
Starting
    application, 5
    automatically, 39
    command, 16-17
    Microsoft Word, 5, 9
    program, 5, 9, 29, 36, 38
    Windows, 2-3
Startup menu, 39
Status bar, 40
Subfolder, 23
Submenu, 9, 16
Switching between
    applications, 10
    programs, 10
    windows, 10

T

Tab key, 20
Taskbar, 3, 5, 10, 11, 39
Text box, 18
Time, 3, 41
Title bar, 8
Toolbar, 40

U

Undeleting a file or folder, 30
Undoing an Explorer action, 29
User profile, 2-3

V

Vertical scroll bar, 13
View, 40

W

Window, 8, 9, 11, 12, 13, 40, 48
Windows NT, v, 2, 3
Windows 95, v, 2, 3, 6
Workgroup, 43
Wizard, 45, 47

"I don't have *time* to figure it out—JUST SHOW ME HOW TO DO IT!"
Windows 95 and NT 4 users in offices everywhere

Sound familiar?

If that's a common plea in your office, then the *Crash Course* books were written just for you (and your co-workers).

Whether you're completely new to the program, converting from another system, or upgrading to Windows 95 or NT 4, you can use each *Crash Course* as your own personal software consultant:

- to get you going FAST
- to answer your questions, on demand
- to point out shortcuts and time-wasters
- to reduce the woes of upgrading
- to get you through your workload without being bogged down by your software

So if you already have more than enough to do at work, don't waste time struggling with your software. The *Crash Course* authors have psyched out the features that lighten your workload. Take advantage of their practical, business-oriented approach, and let the *Crash Courses* be your easy-to-use software guides, starting TODAY!

CRASH COURSE WINDOWS 95 & NT 4.0

Contents

Chapter 1
Essential Windows skills
The desktop • Program and document windows • Menus and commands • Using the Open and Save As commands • Managing folders and files • Windows Explorer

Chapter 2
More useful Windows skills
Shortcuts • Customizing your Start menu • Controlling the view in folder windows • The Control Panel • Local and network drives • Printers and print queues • Online help

2 chapters, 53 pages, **$10**
ISBN 0-911625-97-6

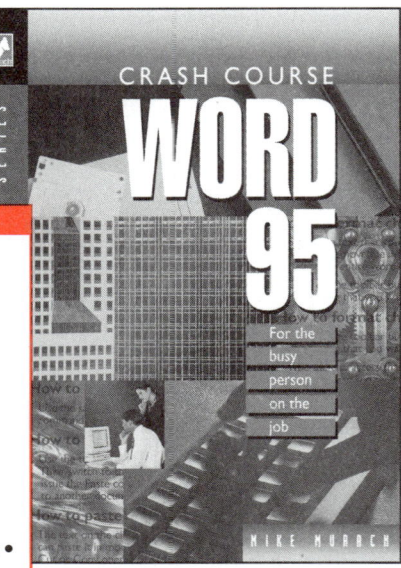

CRASH COURSE EXCEL 95

Contents

Chapter 1
How to create, print, and save a worksheet

Chapter 2
Essential worksheet skills
10 essential editing skills •
10 essential formatting skills •
9 essential skills for working with larger worksheets

Chapter 3
2 features that help you work like a PRO
Working with more than one worksheet at a time • Charts

3 chapters, 83 pages, **$15**
ISBN 0-911625-96-8

CRASH COURSE WORD 95

Contents

Chapter 1
How to create, print, and save a document

Chapter 2
Essential word processing skills
Edit a document • Format characters, paragraphs, and pages • Prepare multi-page documents

Chapter 3
3 features that help you work like a PRO
Templates and wizards • Styles • Tables

3 chapters, 83 pages, **$15**
ISBN 0-911625-95-X

The Murach Crash Courses.
They're faster than asking anyone.

Looking for more than a *Crash Course* in Word or Excel? You'll find what you need in these *Work like a PRO* books

"With any Murach title, a computer user can learn in minutes what would otherwise take hours or days to learn."

**John Skinner
Charlotte Sun Herald**

Our *Crash Courses* on Word and Excel get you going fast with your software. And they may cover every function you'll ever want to use at work.

But if you want to use more advanced or specialized features of these programs…or if you provide support to other PC users…or if you'd like a more extensive reference book…then be sure to take a look at our *Work like a PRO* books. Like this *Crash Course*, the PRO books were written by business users, for business users, so you're always focused on the program features that will help you most at work. And they're set up just like this *Crash Course*, to make learning as painless as possible for you. That means you can:

- Zip through the basics if you're a beginner
- Master more advanced or specialized features whenever you want to
- Find the answers to questions on the spot
- Flip through the book to discover work-saving features you didn't even know existed
- See and experiment with different ways of doing the same function, so you can choose the one that's fastest for you
- Get a crash course in Windows 95 that reduces the woes of upgrading
- Gain confidence…help your co-workers out of trouble when they get stuck…become the office whiz at using Word and Excel!

Each *PRO* book contains all the material that's in the corresponding *Crash Course*, but also covers additional options for some of the *Crash Course* features, along with features that aren't in the *Crash Course* at all. So if you want to move beyond the Word and Excel essentials, be sure to try the *PRO* books TODAY.

Contents

A Crash Course in Windows 95

**Section 1
The essential word processing skills**
Create, print, and save a document • Edit a document • Format characters, paragraphs, and pages • Prepare multi-page documents

**Section 2
The commands and features that help you work like a PRO**
Templates and wizards • Styles • The outline feature • Tables • Tables of contents, lists, footnotes, and endnotes • Columns, graphic objects, and frames • Macros, defaults, file management and conversion, and Word help

**Section 3
How to use the Mail Merge feature**
Mail Merge essentials • Data sources • Other types of main documents

PRO/Word 95, 14 chapters, 369 pages, **$25**
ISBN 0-911625-91-7

Contents

A Crash Course in Windows 95

**Section 1
The essential worksheet skills**
Create, print, and save a worksheet • Edit a worksheet • Format a worksheet • Time-savers for working with larger worksheets

**Section 2
The commands and features that help you work like a PRO**
Working with more than one worksheet at a time • Charts • Advanced formulas and functions • Defaults, data protection, and Excel help • File management and conversion • Templates • Data mapping

**Section 3
How to work with lists and databases**
List essentials • Pivot tables • Using Microsoft Query to access an external database (like an Oracle or Access database)

PRO/Excel 95, 12 chapters, 339 pages, **$25**
ISBN 0-911625-92-5

Not using Windows 95 yet?
Work like a PRO with Word 6 or Excel 5

"These books are superb. At no time while reading either did I ever feel lost or confused: the explanations are concise and lucid, the illustrations are a faithful reproduction of exactly what's on the program screen, and the exercises allowed me hands-on practice to reinforce what I had just read."

**John Kottal
PC User's Group of Colorado**

If you like the approach in this *Crash Course*...if you've found it a painless way to learn...but you're still working in Windows 3.x, then the books on this page are for you. They teach Word 6 and Excel 5 in the same basic way that we've used in this *Crash Course*, so you get all the same benefits:

"The layout makes it easy to view all the relevant information at once (no page flipping)."

Dawn Adams, Trainer

"Gets right to the nitty-gritty by showing you how to use the program features that informed users use to save time."

Mae McConnell, Cherry Hill, New Jersey

"Besides using this book as a beginner's guide to the program, it makes an excellent reference book."

John Broderick, Microcomputer Users Group of Pinellas County

"The book's extensive index and sample screens make it easy to find what you're looking for."

Greg McClure, Winnipeg PC User Group

"This book takes you into some of the real neat things that you can do when working with spreadsheets. It's an excellent book to give to someone who wants to improve their Excel 5 skills."

*Kenneth Mayton,
Central Florida Computer Society*

"I highly recommend this book to all Word 6 users who desire to increase their productivity and versatility in using this program."

Phil Pfeifer, Salem, South Carolina

"Excellent job of presenting the program in more pictures and fewer words."

Gordon Nelson, Gladstone, Michigan

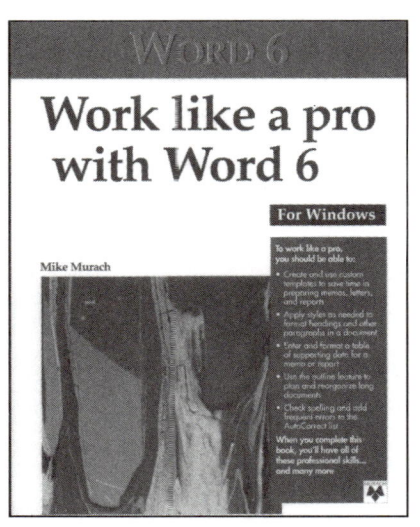

The same functional content as sections 1 and 2 of *Work like a PRO with Word for Windows 95*

PRO/Word 6, 11 chapters, 253 pages, **$20**
ISBN 0-911625-90-9

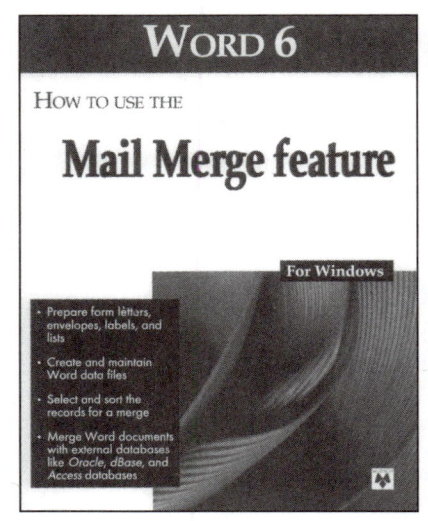

The same functional content as section 3 of *Work like a PRO with Word for Windows 95*

Word 6 Mail Merge, 5 chapters, 71 pages, **$9.95**
ISBN 0-911625-88-7

The same functional content as sections 1 and 2 of *Work like a PRO with Excel for Windows 95*

PRO/Excel 5, 8 chapters, 247 pages, **$20**
ISBN 0-911625-89-5

The same functional content as section 3 of *Work like a PRO with Excel for Windows 95*

Excel 5 Lists, 4 chapters, 60 pages, **$11.95**
ISBN 0-911625-87-9

But you don't have to take anyone's word for it— see for yourself. Get these books and start working like a PRO with Word 6 or Excel 5 today!

Comment Form

Thank you for purchasing this *Crash Course in Windows 95 and NT 4*. If you have any comments, criticisms, or suggestions for us, I'm eager to get them. Your opinions today will affect our products tomorrow. And if you find any errors in this book, typographical or otherwise, please point them out so we can correct them in the next printing.

Thanks for your help.

Mike Murach

Dear Mike:

_____
_____
_____
_____
_____
_____
_____
_____
_____
_____
_____
_____
_____
_____
_____
_____
_____
_____

Order Form

Our Ironclad Guarantee

To our customers who order directly from us: You must be satisfied. Our books must work for you, or you can send them back for a full refund...no questions asked.

Quantity Discounts

Quantity	Discount
10-24	10%
25-99	20%
100-249	25%
250-999	30%
1000-1999	32%
2000-4999	34%

To order more quickly,
Call toll-free 1-800-221-5528
(Weekdays, 8 to 5 Pacific Time)
Fax: 1-209-275-9035

Mike Murach & Associates, Inc.
2560 West Shaw Lane, Suite 101
Fresno, California 93711-2765
(209) 440-9071

Name (& Title, if any) _____
Company (if company address) _____
Street address _____
City, State, Zip _____
Phone number (including area code) _____
Fax number (if you fax your order to us) _____

Qty	Product code and title	*Price
_____	C95N Crash Course in Windows 95 & NT 4.0	$10.00
_____	CCW7 Crash Course in Word 95	15.00
_____	CCX7 Crash Course in Excel 95	15.00
_____	PRW7 Work Like a PRO with Word for Windows 95	25.00
_____	PRMW Work like a PRO with Word 6 for Windows	20.00
_____	MWMM Word 6: How to use the Mail Merge feature	9.95
_____	PRX7 Work like a PRO with Excel for Windows 95	25.00
_____	PREX Work like a PRO with Excel 5 for Windows	20.00
_____	EXLS Excel 5: How to work with lists, pivot tables, & external databases	11.95

❍ Bill me for the books plus UPS shipping and handling (and sales tax within CA).
❍ Bill my company. P.O.# _____
❍ I want to **SAVE 10%** by paying in advance.
   Charge to my ___Visa ___MasterCard ___American Express:
   Card number _____
   Valid thru (mo/yr) _____
   Cardowner's signature _____
❍ I want to **SAVE 10% plus shipping and handling.** Here's my check for the books minus 10% ($_____). California residents, please add sales tax to your total. (Offer valid in U.S.)

*Prices are subject to change. Please call for current prices.

BUSINESS REPLY MAIL
FIRST-CLASS MAIL   PERMIT NO. 3063   FRESNO, CA

POSTAGE WILL BE PAID BY ADDRESSEE

NO POSTAGE
NECESSARY
IF MAILED
IN THE
UNITED STATES

Mike Murach & Associates, Inc.
2560 W SHAW LN STE 101
FRESNO CA 93711-9866